WHEN THE GODS RETURN

by Jack Barranger

THE BOOK TREE
San Diego, California

© 2014 Jack Barranger
All rights reserved

No part of this publication may be used or transmitted in any way without the expressed written consent of the publisher, except for short excerpts for use in reviews.

ISBN 978-1-58509-143-0

Cover art copyright by
Esteban De Armas

Cover layout by
Mike Sparrow

Published by
The Book Tree
P O Box 16476
San Diego, CA 92176

www.thebooktree.com

We provide fascinating and educational products to help awaken the public to new ideas and information that would not be available otherwise.
Call 1 (800) 700-8733 for our FREE BOOK TREE CATALOG.

CONTENTS

Introduction..5

Chapter One
The Hope for an Alien Landing...................................15

Chapter Two
The Reality of an Alien Landing..................................21

Chapter Three
The Devastating Impact of Ancient Religion.......................... 35

Chapter Four
Alien Abductions..47

Chapter Five
A Possible Alien Horror: Cattle and other Animal Mutilations.......59

Chapter Six
Crop Circles...67

Chapter Seven
The Miracle of Fatima:
The Aliens' 20th Century Grand Deception..........................75

Chapter Eight
The Ancient Aliens' Devastating Conditioning: The Slave Chip...83

Chapter Nine
Concerns and Conclusions...93

Appendix One
Why I Believe that the Aliens are Here 101

WHEN THE GODS RETURN
Book Four of the Past Shock series

OTHER BOOKS BY JACK BARRANGER

PAST SHOCK: The Origin of Religion and Its Impact on the Human Soul
(Vol. One of Past Shock series)

THE ORIGIN OF RELIGION AND ITS IMPACT ON THE HUMAN SOUL: Past Shock Part Two

FREEDOM FROM RELIGION: Past Shock Part Three

MYSTERIES EXPLORED: The Search for Human Origins, UFOs, and Religious Beginnings, with Paul Tice.

THE LEGACY OF ZECHARIA SITCHIN, by M.J. Evans; Appendix by Jack Barranger, reprinted from his original booklet of same title.

RICO'S IRREVERENT BIBLE STUDIES: Fifteen Outrageous Lessons You Never Learned in Sunday School

KNOWING WHEN TO QUIT, Second Edition, 2011, originally published by Impact Publishers, 1988.

All of the above titles are available from The Book Tree

Introduction

On February 26 and 27th of 2011, I attended a conference dealing with aliens in ancient history. I was excited about this conference because I had dealt with this subject in my book *Past Shock: The Origin of Religion and Its Impact on the Human Soul*. There I explored the concept that the gods of ancient history were in fact historical beings and they – according to the Holy Bible and other ancient writings – didn't treat us very well.

I went to the conference with high expectations and was disappointed. The speakers avoided any reference to ancient religion and focused mainly on the impressive technology that the aliens left behind. This subject was impressive – but not impressive enough to bring back more than a fraction of the audience on the following day. I attended the event that next day and was disappointed. During an open mike session, I finally decided to make a comment to Georgio Tsoukalos – one of the creators of the *Ancient Aliens* series on television's History Channel.

He inspired the title of this book when he answered someone with: "That will be proven when the gods return."

I went up to the microphone and said, "I don't want the gods to return. They treated us very badly and gave us religion so that they could control us."

Giorgio replied, "Religion was not an alien creation; it was a human invention. Ancient beings had nothing to do with religion."

I was shocked. My years of research showed otherwise. I brought up to him the many atrocities of the ancient god Jehovah and mentioned the flagrant destruction of the Tower of Babel; however, he would not budge. After going back and forth with him for about a minute, I finally said, "On this issue we're going to have to agree to disagree." He did thank me for my question. I thought things over that night and decided to take my case to some of the people who were at the sparsely attended second day of the conference. There I encountered some comments that were so bad that I could not believe them.

Calvin, a large African-American man, told me that, "The most important thing is love. That is what the aliens will teach us – how to love. Nothing else is really relevant. It's all about love."

Norm, a man who had come to the microphone and spoken about the oppressiveness of religion (to the point where I went over and shook his hand afterwards) decided that he didn't want to talk about the oppressiveness of religion. Instead, he decided that he wanted to give a long rant about the oppressiveness of California's governor Jerry Brown. All my attempts to steer the conversation back to the oppressiveness of ancient religion were futile. Norm couldn't get off of his anti governor Brown rant.

Meanwhile I was getting increasingly bad vibes from Calvin's girlfriend. She would look away every time I asked her a question. She absolutely refused to make eye contact with me. This gave me a really creepy feeling. Finally, I made the statement that caused everyone to look at me disapprovingly. "If the gods come back, I'm going to find the nearest cave and hide."

The looks I got were what I would have expected if I had mentioned how much I enjoyed beating my dog to death. I definitely was not among allies here.

Bill, Cancer and the Space Brothers

This disappointing conference was not the only thing to cause me great concern. Bill,* one of my closest friends, recently struggled with cancer. Even during the time of his cancer, he and his wife reached out to me when I was going through an illness. He, after surviving surgery, convinced himself that before coming into life, he had decided to have these experiences so that he could grow as a soul. I had a problem with that. As a survivor of two heart attacks and open-heart surgery, I considered my health issues to be among the low points of my life and refuse to believe that before I was born, I chose them in advance.

[*NOTE: Bill died from cancer in the prime of his life. We met as counselors at the National Music Camp in Interlochen, Michigan in 1961. Our friendship laster for these 43 years. He believed that all aliens were "love and light." As you shall see from reading this book, I had a totally different opinion.]

Bill firmly believes in aliens. He refers to them as "The Space Brothers." He believes that the aliens are going to pick him up sometime soon. He sees the space brothers as nothing but goodness and light and firmly believes that they mean him no ill. I would say that he needs to read my book *Past Shock*, but the problem is that he has already read it *and* the sequel – *The Origin of Religion and Impact on the Human Soul*. Despite having read these two books, he still believes that there are good aliens and bad aliens. He believes that the good aliens are going to win against the bad ones sometime this year. Then they will land and save us from ourselves.

This is a mentality that got me down at the Ancient Aliens conference.

For me to believe that there is such a thing as aliens is a stretch, but I believe. To believe that there are good aliens and bad aliens is also a stretch. I have less of a problem believing in bad aliens than I do good aliens. History and mythology support the idea of bad aliens, but have very little to say about good ones. As I said at the conference, if there is an alien landing, I am going to hide somewhere. UFO researcher John Lear said it very aptly: "If you see a UFO land, run like hell."

The Deception of Channeled Aliens

Channeling is a New Age phenomenon that was the rage a few years ago. When the space brothers are "channeled," one goes into a light trance and begins channeling messages from some of them that are supposedly hovering around the Earth in UFOs. Here is a sample of some of their channeling:

> We are hovering over your planet in the spaceship Zarchon. Soon we will land and save you from the calamities that will soon be upon you. You must not fear these coming calamities because they are meant to be part of your spiritual growth.

> As we hover above you we are overjoyed to see the spiritual progress you are making. As we monitor your Earth plane we are most happy with this progress.

Well, come on, space brothers, are you coming or not coming? Based on biblical and mythological accounts of the flood, you didn't do much to help us then. In the Sumerian *Enuma Elish*, you just sat in your spaceships and watched us drown. And what do you mean by "spiritual progress" anyway? As far as your own progress is concerned, you can color me unimpressed.

I did a lot of research in this area because things can sometimes go too far when certain New Age ideas are unproven. In my (currently) unpublished book *The New Age Nightmare*, I attended about a dozen different channeling sessions and asked the following question of the "space brothers":

"How long ago was there a continent of Atlantis?"

The answers I received ranged from 1200 years ago to twelve million years ago. I did not receive the same answer twice. These channeled beings ranged from "space brothers" to "beings of light" who have never been in a body before. Why should I take seriously some "light being" who has never experienced the horrors of junior high school? Or other more serious challenges we must encounter in life that allows us to *understand* it?

Here is more of the space brothers channeling:

> Soon we will be landing [*They've been saying that since the 1950's.*] Because of the light that we see on your planet we up here in space singing a heavenly chorus of joy because of your spiritual progress. [*Hey, space brothers, have you been to a New Age conference lately?*] We sense the good vibrations that manifested through your spiritual and personal growth. [*I experienced more personal and spiritual growth from the students I taught than I have ever received from a channeling session.*] We hope that you will greet us with open arms when we finally land. [*I'm personally not holding my breath, but if the day comes that you finally do land, my arms are going to be swinging (and my legs pumping) as I run like hell.*]

French UFO researcher Jacques Valle figured out that based on the channeling of the space brothers, there had to be at least 30,000 earthlike planets in the universe, and they are all visiting us. He announced this figure in 1978!

One thing that the space brothers are *not* is consistent.

The New Age Movement

As mentioned before, I wrote a book called *The New Age Nightmare*. It was never published. I was hoping that some Christian publisher would take it and run with it. At the time, I was a born again Christian and a graduate of a Bible-believing seminary. I turned to New Age thought because I believed that it offered an alternative to the oppressiveness of my born again Christian "beliefs."

The New Age movement, however, is rife with cosmic foo-foo. Its present material centers more on wishful thinking than reality.

If one attends a typical New Age weekend conference, one finds a vast over-choice of booths that promise everything from helping you find your cosmic soul mate to the latest homeopathic remedy that will help you lose twenty pounds without feeling a pang of hunger. In another booth you will find channelings from the newest "in" group of the space brothers. Next to it will be a booth of people claiming to have been contacted by the aliens from Zeta Reticuli, promising their imminent return. The fact that the people in these two booths do not get along is one of the mysteries of the New Age movement.

The problem with some – but not all – New Age people is that they can be long on making promises but short on their delivery. New Age people can be rude, yet if you call them on it they will tell you that you have a high level of attachment. Born again Christians will tell anyone who will listen that the New Age movement is being run by the Devil. I assure you that the Devil – if there were indeed one – would not waste his time on something as ineffective as the New Age Movement.

One of the *most* ineffective elements of the New Age Movement lies in the area of aliens (from outer space, not Mexico). There is an almost universal belief that these are the "good guys." New Age people do admit that bad aliens exist. However, they assure us that the good ones are going to win and that we have nothing to fear. The problem with that mentality is in the research of the past. Back then the good aliens hardly existed. As you read through this book, you will encounter documented horror stories that portray the aliens for what they were: mean s.o.b.s. Even the biblical Jehovah is exposed for the psychotic "god" that he was (more on this later).

When I ask New Age people why they think their beliefs are valid, they tell me that they are accepting them "on faith." This is what born again Christians do with Jesus, Roman Catholics do with the Virgin Mary, and Jews do with Jehovah. This book will attempt to convince you that there are very few good aliens. I do not base my views on faith, but upon evidence of what they did to us in the past and what they are doing to us now. Later chapters about alien abductions and cattle mutilations will present evidence instead of naively asking you to accept things on faith. I am going to take the empirical rather than the purely metaphysical approach. The space brothers – if they exist at all – will be shown for what they were and who they are now. This consistent pattern is not revealed in other books, as far as I know.

Some of you may wonder why I used the term "nightmare" in my book *The New Age Nightmare*. Much of what I saw in the New Age Movement was frightening. One example happened during a channeling of the space brothers, when the one channeling the information went totally out of control. The channeler ranted on about how people from Earth were "unconscious scum." He went on to say that we, as citizens of planet Earth, didn't deserve to be saved. In fact, he asserted, we all deserved to die in the coming earth changes (earthquakes, floods, volcanoes, etc.). Finally, the alleged spirit of Jesus Christ came through and continued the harangue. "Jesus," our savior, mentioned that we were all deserving of hellfire and he would spit us out when we approached him. He would have gone on with this terrible rant had I and another person not shouted him down. People who were not bothered by the channeling gave us the dirtiest looks. (How dare we shout down Jesus Christ? Jesus H. Christ, how can you be so insensitive!)

I left the Ancient Aliens conference with the same despondent feeling I had with this channeler. However, that evening I got the idea for this book. The following day, I ran the idea past my publisher and told him how I believed the aliens were up to their old tricks again. In my projected book, I would even take us into the future where I speculate how they will treat us then. The gods (the aliens) are not our friends. They have proven that they are up to no good when it comes to relationships with humans. In the past, they treated us horribly. A close reading of the sacred texts from most any culture will prove it.

This book is meant to be alchemical in a certain sense. I have always considered myself a literary alchemist: I could take bad situations (lead) and turn them into opportunities (gold). I did that when I found myself in a horrible job in Texas and turned that into gold by writing my top selling book, *Knowing When to Quit*. I did it again when I took my religious conditioning and turned it into *Freedom from Religion*. Both of these books are available from the publisher of this book, The Book Tree. And now I am taking an idea that was shot down at a major UFO conference and proving its point – to the best of my ability.

If you don't believe there's such a thing as aliens, then good – I can understand that. I didn't either until I saw a UFO land. Even then I was able to convince myself that this must have been an advanced military experiment. Then I started going to UFO conferences and learned about cattle mutilations and alien abductions and I was convinced – but just barely. My interviews with people who claimed they were abducted pushed me over the edge. I hoped the aliens were the good guys until I started doing research for my book *Past Shock*. Then I realized I couldn't write off these abductees as being crazy and misguided. In fact, all of them were professional people who appeared to be quite reasonable – other than the fact that during some nights aliens would come and take them away.

My hope is that this book will help you see more clearly what we might one day be facing on Planet Earth. If the gods do come again, openly, as they had in the ancient past, then the same negative treatment that was experienced then, will happen again in the future.

Chapter One

The Hope for an Alien Landing

In the New Age community there are high hopes that the aliens will eventually land their UFOs and save us from ourselves. This hope is based upon the assumption that we – as a planet – have lost the ability to sanely run our affairs and that we need outside intervention. As I write this, the world is in turmoil in a number of areas and will continue to be in turmoil when you read this. My good friend Bill cannot understand why the aliens haven't landed sooner and hopes they will land soon.

Should the aliens land, one would hope they would be treated as heroes. They would appear as our saviors, and perhaps even claim that they are on a mission from God. They would of course extend great love and make claims about how they are here to protect and serve us.

The channeled beings tell us that this is a very difficult planet to experience life. We who live here are considered to be heroes by these space brothers. According to these channeled entities, the first thing the landed aliens intend to do is dissolve all governments and wipe out all land borders. They tell us that we are all "citizens of the earth," and claim this is the way that it was intended to be.

One of these channelers brought forth the following message:

Citizens of planet Sargon. [*That is what they call Earth. They don't even have the courtesy to call it by how we name it – much like we in the West insist on calling Deutschland Germany.*] The final days are upon you; we await the call to lift all into our mighty ships, which have been hovering above you, unseen for eons. Your days of suffering will continue only for a short time." [*This message was transmitted in 1982. What exactly do the aliens mean when they say "a short time?"*]

What if a landing really does happen and the entire world gets infused with new energy? The feeling of optimism will be very high within the communities that believe them. A general feeling of optimism would most definitely pervade the planet. Old discords will seem irrelevant, and a feeling of brotherhood will finally infuse the planet. Neighbors who bitterly fought with each other will now embrace one another. What appeared to be serious problems in the past will fall away and be replaced with this higher spirit of optimism.

The landed aliens will promise that a new day is coming and that people can finally live in peace. Bitter civil wars will suddenly end with the establishment of a kind of interplanetary U.N. force. Boards established by the aliens will resolve political battles. The media will display a common group of governing aliens whom they will swear hold an uncommon wisdom. Children of all races and ethnic backgrounds will play freely and happily with each other. People who never had anything in common will now join arms and end up singing songs together. At first, a few people will be cynical and suspicious, but they will quickly be won over by the charm and sincerity of the aliens.

With the promise of international citizenship, most people will be willing to accept the dissolving of their national borders. While there will be a few "holdouts," eventually a high number of Earth's people will be won over.

The aliens who monitor the schools may look strange; however there will be an overall good feeling about them. Students in junior high school who were fiercely bullied will find their bulliers to be more docile and not at all threatening. Teasing and bullying will be a thing of the past and overweight children will no longer feel pressure to conform to "right body" images. Teachers will all be listened to with an uncommon attention from students and will often be thanked for their time and dedication by parents and students alike.

People in churches will at first be skittish about the aliens. Some will initially feel that they will be agents of the devil. However, they will be somewhat reassured when the aliens tell them that they represent the creator of the universe and that there are many paths to discovering the true God. The many factions of Christianity will be explained as being acceptable pathways to truth. The aliens will claim that Moses, Mohammad, and Jesus all provided a pathway to God and that God does not have a desire to harshly judge anyone. Those who are convinced that God will judge those of a different faith than theirs'– or no faith at all – will now begin to mellow and accept what the aliens will say. The fact that they have a greater technological superiority will go a long way toward convincing people to accept the idea of the universality of all faiths. Protestants will show up in Roman Catholic churches and join hands in a warm solidarity, in addition to other faiths intermingling as well. TV coverage will eventually free itself of its current negative images and its continued violence will wane. The aliens will claim, just like the channeled messages that we hear today claim, that this planet is a school for learning lessons.

There is just one problem with this scenario: it's not going to happen this way. In fact, history teaches us much about the future. Based on what ancient history tells us, when the aliens openly land, we can expect nowhere near the scenario as outlined above, but a nightmare. Just look at our own behavior, for example. Whenever mankind has moved into any new area, those who were native to it are first exploited, then subjugated, then completely conquered and finally, often become victims of genocide – as long as the interlopers were superior technologically or militarily. This is our own clear historical pattern. If we have anything here on this planet that the aliens might want, which would give them a purpose to travel here in the first place, then there is no reason why it should not be their pattern as well.

I am simply offering the world a warning when everyone might otherwise be so happy to see a new era dawning with the coming of the "gods." Watch out for Trojan horses.

Channeled messages should all be suspect because in order trust *any* information, one should always be completely certain of the source. Hearsay and real proof are two different things. Some New Age people will wax lyrical about the channeling phenomenon. I am not that impressed. The fact that many of the "spirits" claim to be of alien origin does not aid the cause of realizing that we might have aliens in our midst. In fact, their inane – and often insane – pronouncements actually throw a monkey wrench of confusion into people's paradigms.

Sadly, no channeled alien spirit has brought much clarity to the alien issue. Instead, they have only muddied the waters. Perhaps, in the spirit of a "someone is messing with us" mentality, this is their intention. As far as providing proof that we have an alien presence on this planet, channeling has done more harm than good.

The channeling by alleged alien beings may be inconsistent; however, it is constant. If there are indeed no such things as aliens then we are deluding ourselves in a mighty way, and allowing channeled spirits to dominate our lives. They may have no real concept of time (i.e. the fact that twelve different "channeled" beings claimed that Atlantis existed anywhere from 1200 to 1,200,000 years ago makes one wonder if the alien educational system is even worse than ours). We must treat channeled messages from so-called aliens – or from spirits of any kind – with suspicion. If the gods are coming back, I personally don't believe we'll hear about it, at least with any accuracy, from some kind of channeled message.

Chapter Two

The Reality of an Alien Landing

The idea of this planet being a school might feel good to some. However, it is not very realistic. Nothing in our ancient history or what is being done by aliens in the present time (like abductions) supports it. In this chapter we will explore what the aliens did to us in our ancient past. While I might have some doubts about whether or not aliens are with us today, I have no doubt about the fact that aliens were with us thousands of years ago.

In fact, I explored this in my book *Past Shock*. Thousands of years ago – perhaps hundreds of thousands years ago – aliens were here on this planet mining for gold. To avoid a mutiny among the disgruntled workers, they created humans as a slave race to work in the mines. When this human slave race began to rebel, the aliens had to do something desperate to quell the rebellion. At first, they used the threat of punishment. When this didn't work, they finally created religion and the threat of eternal damnation as a means to control the people and get them to work hard. The idea was that if one worked hard in this life, one could expect rest and reward for eternity. This evidently worked, and we are still carrying around that mentality today. Although my opinions on this matter might be hard to accept, it can be further explored and backed up with research in books like *Past Shock* and Zecharia Sitchin's

The Twelfth Planet, among dozens of others.

Into this ancient reality came one of the most despicable characters from ancient history: the "god" Jehovah. Jehovah was not God—although he after proclaimed in Stentorian fashion that he was. He could get very mean with people who didn't believe in his claimed standing, and often did devastating things, and caused humans to do devastating things in his name. When a man dared to pick up sticks on the Sabbath, he insisted that this man be stoned to death. When a man was caught making love to a woman from another tribe, Jehovah insisted on the same punishment. When he made a "covenant" with the Jewish people, it came out like "my way or the highway" more than any negotiated agreement. These examples all come from *The Holy Bible*.

Jehovah's Despicable Covenant

I referred to this in *Past Shock* as "an offer we couldn't refuse." It began with Jehovah appearing to be a compassionate god:

> If you follow my laws and faithfully observe my commandments, I will grant you rains in their seasons so that the earth will yield its produce and the trees of the field their fruit. Your threshing shall overtake the vintage, and the vintage shall overtake the sowing; you will eat your fill of bread and dwell securely in your land. I will grant peace in the land, and you will

> be untroubled by anyone. I will give the land respite from vicious beasts, and no sword shall cross your land. You shall give chase to your enemies, and they shall fall beside you by the sword. I will look with favor upon you and make you fertile and multiply you, and I will maintain my covenant with you. You shall eat grain long stored...
>
> —Leviticus 26: 3-10

You have to admit that this sounds like a good deal. But wait, it suddenly gets worse:

> But if you do not obey me and do not follow these commandments, if you reject my laws and spurn my norms so that you do not follow my commandments and break my covenant, I in turn will do this to you. I will wreak misery upon you – consumption and fever, which will cause the eyes to pine and the body to languish; you shall sow your seed to no purpose, for your enemies shall eat it. I will set my face against you; you shall be routed by your enemies, and your foes shall dominate you. You shall flee though none pursues.
>
> —Leviticus 26: 14-17

The good deal doesn't look so good anymore. This is not a freely negotiated agreement. It is more the words of a bully than a compassionate God. This is more like a warlord claiming to be God.

The situation continues to get worse. At this point Jehovah is only able to speak in negatives:

> And for all of you that do not obey me, I will go on disciplining you seven-fold for your sins....
> —Leviticus 26: 18

Seven-fold? Isn't that a bit much, Mr. Jehovah?

The covenant continues to deteriorate:

> I will break your proud glory. I will make the skies like iron and your earth like copper, so that your strength shall be spent to no purpose. Your land will not yield its produce, nor shall the trees yield their fruit.
> —Leviticus 26: 19-20

At no point did Jehovah consider this to be cruel and unusual punishment. It is almost as if he is expecting his "chosen people" to "sin." Although this may sound redundant, this covenant actually does get worse:

> I will loose wild beasts against you, and they shall bereave you of your children, and wipe out your cattle... and if you withdraw into your cites, I will send pestilence among you, and you shall be delivered into enemy hands… You shall eat the flesh of your sons and the flesh of your daughters.
>
> —Leviticus 26: 22-29

Can you imagine being so hungry that you would have to eat the flesh of your children? How about your brothers and sisters? What Jehovah lacked in compassion and good taste he made up for with a vivid imagination. In this covenant the punishment far exceeded the "crime." This is one example of the alien mentality we might expect to return someday. Why should it be any different? Remember that this covenant occurred after "God" wiped out humanity with the great flood, which occurred after the destruction of the Tower of Babel.

The Heinous Destruction of the Tower of Babel

Many events in the history of humanity actually go beyond description as low points. One of these was the burning of the library at Alexandria. Here, a repository of the world's greatest knowledge was destroyed on the whim of a Christian fanatic, Philo. Another historical low point is mentioned in the Bible; however, it only gets a few verses – that being the destruction of the Tower of Babel.

Most Jews and Christians are falsely led to believe that "God" had to destroy the temple because his people were arrogant and had overstepped their bounds. A closer scrutiny of these few verses however sheds a different light on the event. Evidently, members of the highly intelligent human race decided to build a city. It was a beautiful city, and the humans were proud of their work and wanted to share it with the known world. Since the aliens were the creators of the human race, they should have been proud that humans had done something like this and complimented them for it. Instead, the highly insecure group of ancient aliens were threatened and determined that this present group of humans had become too smart for their own good. Instead of rewarding these humans, they decided to "dumb them down."

> Let us go down and confound their language....
> —Genesis 11:7

The ancient aliens not only made it so that the humans could not understand each other, but also scattered them all over the planet.

This was a despicable act. Those who think that the present aliens would be any different today are hopelessly deluding themselves. Today's aliens would be highly threatened by humans who showed advanced levels of intelligence. They couldn't scatter us all over the earth because we are already scattered all over the earth. However, thanks to the aliens' ancient conditioning, through the Tower of Babel "confusion of tongues program," we now speak thousands of languages and dialects and for this reason still have a hard time understanding one another.

The ancient Mayan scripture, the *Popul Vuh*, speaks of a time in ancient history when the gods were concerned that humanity was too intelligent and didn't want to work that hard for them. They (the gods) were also concerned that humanity would not worship and venerate them:

> We have already tried with our first creations, our first creatures, but not make them praise and venerate us. So let us try to make obedient, respectful beings who will nourish and respect us.
> —*Popul Vuh*

Eventually the experiment yielded unexpected results:

> ...they saw instantly and could see far, they succeeded in seeing, they succeeded in knowing, where all is in the world. When they looked, they saw instantly all around them, and contemplated in turn the arch of the heaven and the round face of the earth.
> —*Popul Vuh*

This was written at a time when the earth was considered to be flat, It must have been most disturbing to their creators who only wanted creatures who would praise and venerate them.

Not only were the ancient aliens insecure, but they were also petty. The ancient Sumerian god Enlil has the following complaint:

> Their conjugations [massive voices complaining]
> do rob me of sleep.
>
> —*Atra Hasis*

Enlil, according to the *Atra Hasis,* eventually solved the problem by bringing on the flood (evidently allowing a flood to happen without warning the humans), which almost totally destroyed the human race. Enki, from his compassion, warned Utnapishtim (Noah) of the impending disaster and was able to save a small portion of the human race. When Enlil was watching the flood from the safety of his space ship, he actually shed a tear and claimed that he would indeed miss the humans. When Enki told Enlil what he had done with warning Utnapishtim, Enlil went into a rage.

This is representative of what the ancient aliens did with humans. Enlil was eventually able to sleep, but it came at a very steep price. What proof do we have that the aliens would be any more compassionate today?

The *Book of Enoch* reveals the conditioning inflicted upon the emerging humans:

> And to Gabriel the lord said: 'You must take action against the bastard children who have become reprobates – the children of fornication, Destroy all the children of The Watchers [the ancient aliens] and set them against one another so that they will kill each other in battle: for they have not long life. And no pleading, which the fathers shall make, shall be listened to. And when their sons have killed each other and they have witnessed the destruction of their loved ones, imprison them for seventy years in the valley of the lowlands until the day of their trial. Then they shall be led off into the Ravine of Fire where they will be imprisoned for life.
>
> —The Book of Enoch 10: 1-12

Here we see the ancient aliens using humans as chattel –to fight their (the aliens) wars. This is most likely what we would experience from the aliens today. We don't see any problems fighting wars in foreign lands. If the landed aliens today requested that we fight wars for them, we would most likely go along. This is what the ancient aliens requested in the past, and they would most likely expect us to do that now.

The Book of Enoch is not canon (books which were chosen to be in the Bible); however, it was strongly considered in church councils to be considered as scripture. It narrowly escaped making the cut. Many trusted scholars and references state that this was the most widely read book by Christians during the first two centuries after Christ.

A survey of early church history reveals that many of the books that are now scripture barely made it in. Martin Luther, the backbone of the Protestant Reformation, wanted the Book of Revelation removed for the New Testament and replaced with the non-canonical *Apocalypse of Peter*. Here Jesus makes a journey into Hell and finds everyone – including all of the Old Testament prophets – stuck there. They ask Jesus to free them from their plight.

The *Book of Enoch* goes even further. Evidently, Enoch's alien-led tour took him to some terrible places:

> From there I was taken to a place that was even more horrible, and I saw another fearsome thing: a great fire which burned and blazed in a place which was cleft down to the ravine, full of great, falling columns of fire. I could neither see its size nor its extant; nor could I even guess at them. I said, "How fearful is this place and how terrible to look at."

This was Enoch's conditioning by the ancient aliens. What could lead us to believe that the aliens would treat us any differently today? The aliens chose Enoch because he demonstrated a superb ability to write vividly. Yet during his tours he spent most of his time being terrified:

> I entered the house, and it was as hot as fire and cold as ice, and it was devoid of comfort. And I began to panic again, and to tremble.
> —The Book of Enoch 16: 13-14

Enoch was a "chosen one" of the ancient aliens. Imagine how they treated common humans and people they didn't like. Can we expect them to be any different today?

A Petty Jehovah

Jehovah could be amazingly harsh when people complained or dared to find someone else to worship. If someone insulted one of his prophets we find situations that transpire like this:

> And he [the prophet Elisha] went up to Bethel, and as he was going up by the way, there came forth little children out of the city, and mocked him, and said unto him, "Go up thou bald head, go up thou bald head."
> —Second Kings 2:23

Perhaps their mistake was saying it two times. If they had only said it once, Jehovah might have shown them mercy. But he didn't. Jehovah was a very petty and vicious god. The next verse shows how low Jehovah eventually stooped:

> And he [Elisha] turned back, and looked back, and cursed them in the name of the Lord. And there came forth two she bears out of the wood, and tare forty and two of them.
> —Second Kings 2:24

It was a brutal attack. In effect, it was as if Jehovah was saying, "That'll teach you to mess with my prophets, you little shits." Come on, Jehovah, isn't this a tad overreacting?

Isn't this just a bit excessive? The children were not putting Elisha's life in danger. They were not inflicting any physical pain upon him. They were simply teasing him. Yet the children experienced a horrible death.

Evidently, Jehovah was also into cannibalism:

> And the king said unto her, 'What aileth thee?' and she answered, "this Woman said unto me, 'Give thy son that we might eat him today, and we will eat my son tomorrow.' So we boiled my son and did eat him. And I said unto her on the next day, give thy son that we might eat him.
> —Second Kings: 6:28

Ladies and gentlemen, this is the *Holy Bible* I am quoting from.

The Prophet Jeremiah even got into this mentality.

> And I will cause them to eat the flesh of their sons and the flesh of their daughters, and they shall eat everyone the flesh of their friend.
> —Jeremiah 19: 9

This is what happened in our ancient past. Can we expect that, if these so-called "gods" were to return today, that they would act any differently? Or force us, as their faithful followers, to act any differently?

Chapter Three

The Devastating Impact of Ancient Religion

If there is one thing the planet would be better off without, it is organized religion. More people have been killed in the name of organized religion than in secular wars in all of history. The subtitle of my book *Past Shock* is *The Origin of Religion and Its Impact on the Human Soul.* There I more deeply explain how the aliens gave us organized religion as a means of controlling us. We have no reason to believe that the aliens who were here before would not resort to using the same methods of control, should they ever come back today. In fact, since the aliens left thousands of years ago, we have done an excellent job of continuing that conditioning on our own. That's how powerful it was.

When believers sing "Gimme that old time religion," they actually mean, "give me that old time oppression."

As mentioned previously, the gods (aliens) were here on Earth mining for gold when they began to rebel against the tedious work. The ancient holy book the *Atra Hasis* gives very clear evidence:

> Let us confront out chief officer, that he might relieve our heavy work.... Excessive toil has killed us. Our work is heavy, the distrust much.
> —Atra Hasis

What ensued were long negotiations. In order to prevent a mutiny, a suggestion was offered:

> Let a Lulu [primitive worker] be created while the birth goddess is present. Let her create a primitive worker. Let him bear the yoke. Let him carry the toil of the gods.
> —Atra Hasis

The goddess was Ninharsag, a Sumerian goddess. Thus a worker was created. We humans are the offspring of that worker race. Because of the potential mutiny among the newly created humans, the gods had to come up with something more effective to combat the possible threat. That turned out to be the creation of religion. This process has now lasted for thousands of years. We were taught to worship the gods we were working for. In fact, as author Paul Tice once pointed out, the original Sumerian word for "worship" actually meant "to work for." These functions were basically one and the same. After the toil stopped, we merely gave reverence to the gods and that alone became our "worship."

At one time on planet Earth we were without organized religion. We worked in the mines for gold – for the aliens. When we rebelled against the oppressiveness and meniality of the tasks, the aliens searched for ways to control us. The aliens tried many different "experiments" (including biological experiments). Once they had figured out how to create a worker that was smart enough to do the needed labor, and stupid enough not to rebel quite as easily as they had, they needed to insure that we would stay in line with the program. It was time for organized religion, and the wonderful promises that go with it. They promised the newly created mine workers that if they worked hard in this lifetime, they would get to rest for all eternity. They eventually asked us to worship them as gods and fight their wars for them. The *Old Testament* and other holy books are full of examples.

Even when the humans decided that they wanted to exist peacefully, the gods intervened and made sure they continued fighting battles.

> All of the cities did not attempt to make peace with the children of Israel, with the exception of the Hivites, who lived in Gibeon. Everyone else fought in battle. But the Lord hardened [the Hivites] their hearts so that they would battle with Israel, that Israel might destroy them completely, and that they would find no fortune, but that Israel might destroy them.
> —Joshua 11: 19-20

This is not an isolated example from the *Old Testament*. In the book of *Exodus* we get another example of this "hardening of hearts." Pharaoh has agreed to let Moses and his people go; however Jehovah would have none of that:

> And the Lord said to Moses 'Go to the Pharaoh, for I have hardened his heart and the hearts of his servants that I might show my powers before him.'

Here, a wrathful, vengeful "God" intervened between two men who agreed to peaceful conditions. However, Jehovah wanted to insure that this "wartime theater" would continue.

The Hindu God Krishna experienced the same boredom. In the *Mahabharata*, Arjuna has made peace with his enemy. However, Krishna would have none of that and actually goads Arjuna into fighting a battle which he (Arjuna), because he and his enemy had previously worked out a peace agreement. Despite what happened, they did not have to fight.

Yet the gods insisted on being worshiped as God Almighty and to be worshiped as God. The following is a from a chapter in the *Old Testament*:

> And the Lord spake unto Moses saying, Speak unto all the congregation of the children of Israel and say to them, Ye shall be holy, for I the Lord your God am holy. Ye shall fear every man his mother, and his father, and keep my Sabbaths: I am the Lord your God. Turn ye not unto idols, nor make to yourselves molten gods: I am the Lord your God.
>
> —Leviticus 19:1-4

We are only four verses into the chapter and the speaker to Moses has mentioned that he is indeed the Lord three times. The chapter has thirty-seven verses and he says the equivalent of "I am the true God" more than ten times. (In the King James edition of the bible the word "LORD" is capitalized every time it is used.) This is evidently a highly insecure warlord who has to use repetition and redundancy frequently in order to drive home his point. Hitler once said, "If you tell a lie long enough, people will end up believing it."

Deaths in the Name of Christ

If Jesus did not die on the cross, this means that a large number of people died for something that never happened. This means that all who were put to death by popes and grand inquisitors were killed to support a myth – something which the mass of people still support today without even questioning it.

God (actually Jehovah) caused the deaths of 180,000 of the Israelis while they were sleeping. (At least their deaths were painless.)

Whole troops who dared to worship the "idol" Baal were slaughtered because they had the "wrong" beliefs. But God had given fair warning – he had indicated to the Israeli people that he was a "jealous God." He countless times slaughtered his chosen people for the "crime" of worshiping idols.

The Crusaders (1198-1201), along their journey to and from Jerusalem, murdered their fellow Christians because of their appetite for blood. They not only killed everyone including the children, but also raped the women. This was in addition to the ones the Crusaders killed during the battle for Jerusalem.

Evidently the Muslim warrior Saladin was up to the task and killed many Crusaders in battles, which raged on for three years.

In 1244, Pope Clement ordered the death of all remaining Cathars (a branch of Christians whose beliefs not only followed the precepts of Jesus but also believed that one should cleanse himself to be pure before God; however, they did not believe in Christ's divinity). They were difficult to reach because they were "holed up" in a castle in France called Montsegur. The pope's troops stormed the castle and killed every living being – throwing them into a raging fire. (They, to be fair, did give them a chance to convert to the "true faith" first.) They, to a person, did not convert and were thus thrown into a raging fire below. When I stood at that very spot in 1999, a person from France said to me that this was the spot where the pope's troops "cooked their dinner."

The popes and grand inquisitors ordered the deaths of many "heretics" (a word that derives from the ancient Greek, meaning "to choose.") I guess the "heretics" chose badly.

On Friday the thirteenth of October in 1307, thousands of the Knights Templar, a legendary Christian warrior group, were rounded up and put on trial for heresy. This was brought about by the King of France, Phillip the Fair and grand inquisitor William Imbert. The Templars has become notoriously rich and Phillip wanted their money. William wanted many bodies to burn at the stake for heresy. All of the Templars were put on trial and severely tortured until they confessed to crimes they never committed. When they finally confessed, they were put out of their misery from torture by being burned at the stake. Philip got himself out of debt, and William was sure that he was doing the right thing.

Similar deaths were those of John Hus and Jerome of Prague in the early 1400s. Hus and Jerome were leaders of a group referred to as the Hussites. Martin Luther came a century later to reform the Church once and for all, but Luther himself admitted that without Hus or Jerome, there would have never been a Reformation. They sacrificed themselves, made a huge difference in history, but few people know anything about them. At the Council of Constance (1414-1418) Hus and Jerome were branded as heretics and both were burned at the stake – Hus in 1415 and Jerome of Prague in 1416. Their heresy: wanting the Bible to be translated into Czech, the language of the people, so that people could read the Bible for themselves. They also wished to ban the selling of indulgences, which consisted of the church basically selling free tickets into heaven in exchange for generous donations to the church. During the Council Hus found thirty-three references from scripture which supported his argument for people to be able to read and understand the Bible directly for themselves. The Church would none of it. He was then told that he was to be burned at the stake, and they claimed that he was a heretic. In subsequent years more than 300 Hussites (beyond Jerome of Prague and Hus) were burned at the stake for heresy.

The Jesus Problem

To many people in America, Jesus would not represent a problem at all. We are one of the rare countries in which millions of Christians take their faith so seriously. Realizing this, the aliens have a near perfect set up for controlling us. In the many channeling sessions that go on with the "Space Brothers," reference goes on assuming that Jesus was the Son of God. Some will go as far to claim that Jesus was one of them.

There is just one problem with this: Jesus Christ may never have existed in the way most people think. Evidence continues to come forth showing that this may in fact be true.

Many needless murders happened in his name, yet one is not really sure whether he actually existed at all. This is a bold statement, but let's look at the evidence.

No prominent historian (Tacitus, Pliny the Younger, Suetonius. etc.) of the first four centuries ever mentions Jesus. The exception is Flavius Josephus who allegedly wrote the following:

> Now there was at the time of Jesus, a wise man, if it be lawful to call him a man, for he was a doer of wonderful works, a teacher of such men as receive the truth with pleasure. He drew over to him both many of the Jews and many of the Gentiles. He was the Christ, and when Pilate, at the suggestion of the principal men amongst us, had condemned him to the cross, those who loved him at the first, did not forsake him, for he appeared to them alive again the third day, as the divine prophets had foretold these and ten thousand other wonderful things concerning him. And the tribe of Christians, so named from him, are not extinct so to this day.

The problem is that this is not written in the style of Josephus and is most likely a forgery (something added claiming to be written by the author.) The *coup de grace* is the use of the word "gentiles." This term in the context it was written did not come into existence until long after Josephus died. This particular passage did not appear until well into the fourth century. Earlier editions do not contain this passage.

That leaves us with the four gospels. These were considered, even by conservative scholars, to be written at least fifty years after the alleged Jesus died. And two of the gospels don't even mention Christ's resurrection and ascension, which would have had to be so amazing that historians would be compelled to write about it.

What does this have to do with the aliens – the gods? First, we were originally programmed by the "gods" to believe in things that have little evidence. The gods claimed to be our original creators and the creators of the entire universe, but offered no proof. We still believed it – simply because they said so. Jehovah is one good example, with his boisterous Old Testament claims. But the gods were actually an alien race that tampered with our genetics to alter us in a way that suited their manipulative needs. But we were already here (and so was the universe) when they showed up. So we need to be careful in accepting any dogmatic religious beliefs based only on hearsay, or because "it's in the Bible, so it must be true!"

Today, in many channeling sessions the "aliens" proclaim that Jesus was an alien. Hearsay again. If Jesus did not exist, this could prove to be embarrassing to them. That would also make what happened in Jesus' name – the millions of murders – even more tragic.

We have another problem. When people were writing about Jesus, they were often writing about someone else. History has many crucified and resurrected saviors. Jesus is in no way alone in this area. Many in later history referred to Jesus as the returned pagan God Mithras. Mithraism was very popular in Rome and references to Mithras are strangely connected to Jesus.

Mithras was born on December 25th with a virgin birth, and was visited by shepherds bearing gifts. He eventually chose and preached with 12 companions. He was buried in a tomb and after the passing of three days arose from the dead. He was referred to as "the lamb of God." Also, he was considered "the way, the truth, and the light."

Mithras' followers celebrated his resurrection from the dead once a year in what was to later be known as Easter (a name derived from the goddess Ishtar). He had a last supper in which he instructed his followers to eat of his body and drink of his blood.

Jesus, if he existed at all, was not born on December 25th.

The Hindu god Krishna was also born on December 25th (of a virgin). His birth was announced by a star appearing in the East, and his father was a carpenter. A tyrant of his time ordered all young boys to be slaughtered. He was transfigured in front of his disciples, and he gave these disciples the ability to work miracles. Allegedly, he was crucified between two thieves. He rose from the dead and ascended to heaven in "the sight of all men." Krishna is said to return to judge the quick and the dead. People, at his time, believed him to be the Son of God.

Here we have a Hindu and a Persian "Son of God." The aliens were evidently around during the time of each of them. The Egyptian God Horus (whose eye appears on the back of a one dollar bill) has many traits, which are similar to Jesus. He was also born on December 25th, and his mother was a virgin. At age 12 he taught in the temple. . During his ministry he delivered a sermon on the mount. He performed miracles and exorcized demons. He promised that after his death he would come back and reign for a thousand years. Also, he was crucified between two thieves.

Since the material about Jesus did not appear in any *historical* documents and he was not even referred to in material written by the church fathers until well into the second century, we would not be considered off base if we thought that people in that time thought Jesus might have been Mithras, Krishna, or Horus returned. We might be guilty of heresy (the right to choose what to believe) but we would not be "off base."

Jesus is not even mentioned in the Dead Sea Scrolls (ancient books which were discovered in Israel in 1947). In fact, the scrolls refer to a person known as "The Righteous One." Scholars who have researched the Scrolls claim this must have been Apollonius of Tyana, a person who was considered to be a messiah figure around Jesus' time. Apollonius also performed miracles, and these are recorded in the Dead Sea Scrolls. This was also said about Simon of Perea, killed by the Romans in 4 BC, and reputed to have been resurrected in 3 days.

There is a good reason why we have not been told any of this: the aliens are behind much of the programming that keeps us in line with religion and they have continued to use it to manipulate us. Even if we were told of alternative choices to religion – or the way we accept it – we, for the most part, do not want to believe it anyway. We'd rather be comfortably ignorant than shaken up with the discomfort of truth. We've been programmed this way because the aliens are much more into control than they are into allowing personal freedom. In the ancient past, little evidence exists of beings who wanted to set humanity free. In fact, what the aliens are taking most advantage of is what I call the slave chip, which is what they programmed us with, and which will be discussed more fully in a later chapter.

For now, if there are indeed alien beings visiting us, what they are really doing to us today, behind the scenes and beyond the ancient programming, is another horror story in itself.

Chapter Four

Alien Abductions

No area stirs up controversy like the area of alien abductions. It seems far-fetched at first, but the deeper one probes into the evidence, the more real things seem to become. If abductions are really happening then the title of this book could be referring to the present time. But to clarify, what I mean by the title of this book, is to the time when they *openly* reveal themselves and either ask – or demand – our trust.

In the mid-1990's I received an assignment from *New Perspectives* magazine to write three articles about alien abductions. To claim that I was skeptical of the phenomena would have been an understatement. The research I did for these articles turned out to be a life changing experience.

First of all, what made the articles attractive to Alan Hartley, my editor, was the fact that a Roper Poll claimed that between two and five million people in America thought they were abducted by aliens. I made plans to interview forty people who would claim that they were abducted by aliens. I had to do the interviews in a way that the "abductees" wouldn't sense that they were being interviewed: "alien abductees" are highly distrustful of journalists. That would have ended most interviews immediately. Therefore, I would not take any notes.

My first interview was serendipitous. I was having dinner with a group of people attending a UFO conference. The conversation was most pleasant. Finally someone asked me a question:

"Jack, have you ever been abducted?"

I said no.

"Then you are the only person at this table who hasn't been abducted."

I polled the table, asking the following question:

"Have you ever been abducted by aliens?"

Each person said yes, and I was stunned.

It was then that I began to realize that each alien abductee experiences almost exactly the same thing.

What Happens During an Alien Abduction

First of all, the person is sleeping comfortably when he wakes up and usually finds that he can't move. Then he or she notices that he is not alone in the room. The person has two or more "aliens" in the room with him. These are, for the most part, four to five-foot tall skinny figures that have since been referred to as "the grays." One cannot say, "No thank you" to these creatures. They have a power over one's mind and can make anyone do what they want.

Usually what they want is for you to go with them to a place of their choosing – usually the medical room in their UFO. There, most abductees experience a medical examination, which is usually quite painful. For men, sperm can be extracted by painful suction. For women, a large needle can be thrust into the uterus. Complaints of pain are often ignored. In some rare examples, the pain is stopped – but the examination continues. Strangely enough, a few people state that they have never experienced more love in their life than during this painful abduction (not a common occurrence). This appears to be an extreme example of the Stockholm Syndrome – like what Patty Hearst experienced when she stopped fighting her captors and wanted to become part of their group.

After the examination some of the abductees are then forced to watch a video, which shows Planet Earth being destroyed by pollution or nuclear weapons. All this is happening while they are naked –having not been dressed since their examination. After the video session or medical exam they are returned to their bedrooms – in most cases. Some abductees are returned miles from their home – some with their shoes on the wrong feet. One abductee was terrified to find herself more than twenty miles from her home and at the time had no idea where she was. It causes one to wonder if these aliens sometimes forget where they picked these people up and, in their intense study of human life, they don't know what shoes are or how to put them on. Just remember this should they ever open reveal themselves and demand to be worshipped as gods.

One abductee claimed that he was sexually assaulted. An alien would lie on top of him and provide him with the most violated feeling he had in his life. Another claimed that she woke up with an alien making love to her. In the ancient holy books it was the "fallen angels," not the true God, that were guilty of these infractions.

Most of the people I interviewed, however, had "uneventful" abductions – other than having sperm painfully extracted from them or having a large needle plunging into their uterus. Every one of them had to bear the humiliation of being naked through the entire session.

Just about everyone I talked to experienced problems sleeping after the abduction, and a few discovered small implants placed in their bodies. Most wish they had control over their circumstances; however, none of them knew when the next abduction was coming. With each one of them, the next abduction eventually happened. They just didn't know when it was going to happen.

What Alien Abductees Experience in Society

Most of the people I talked to experienced one main frustration: they can't talk to anyone about what they are experiencing. Just imagine if you said this to a close friend:

> Last night I was abducted by aliens. They took me to their spaceship and made me undress. Then they put me through a very painful medical exam. I was forced to watch a most upsetting

> video of Earth being destroyed by pollution. Then they returned me to my bedroom. I woke up in the morning with this bruise on my leg. It was a horrible experience.

Quite likely, the person hearing this will think that it's a horrible experience having to *listen to you.* Any psychologist or psychiatrist you try to explain your problem to has no choice other than think that you are "whacked out." This explains why abductees form support groups to help them find psychologists like Yvonne Smith – a practicing psychologist in the Los Angeles area who is sympathetic to abductees and will not rush to judgment.

David Jacobs, a history teacher at Temple University, is an author who writes about the abduction phenomena in books like *Secret Life,* and who keeps a list of psychologists and psychiatrists who will treat these people with understanding. The late John Mack, who was head of the Harvard Medical School Department of Psychiatry, also believed that alien abductions were real and had to go before a group of his peers to defend his right to continue talking and speaking at UFO conferences about the problem. He was told that he could continue speaking about these things because his peers feared that a day might come where they would have *their own* rights to speak eventually curtailed. (John was killed by a drunk driver while on a speaking tour in England.)

Some UFO conferences offer support groups for abductees. I don't qualify because as far as I know, I have never been abducted. Thus, when I am at a UFO conference I am unable to continue research in an area of high interest. People who have been abducted claim that they feel safe at a UFO conference and feel that they can say anything and people will not judge them. That is one area where the New Age Movement really shines.

The Aliens' Viewpoint

As far as free will and compassion are concerned, the aliens could care less and have shown no respect toward humans whatsoever. They are going to get what they want, and human feelings be damned. If they actually feel this way now, what are they going to do if they openly land? People's feelings and needs will be ignored on a large planet-wide scale.

In normal life, if you claim you can't sleep at night you get a sleeping pill from your doctor. A very simple answer. But aliens have no ethical code like human doctors do. They treat us like animals. When abducted you might claim that the medical examination hurts, but when have animal research scientists ever considered the pain of the animals they are experimenting on? The aliens are going to put these implants inside of you whether you like it or not. Should they decide that they are going place "implants" inside you, you cannot stop them. They are going to do exactly what they want, and nothing is going to stop them. Human values be damned. To them we are nothing more than cattle.

As explained in this book and in my *Past Shock* trilogy, our ancient past was a horror story. How ironic that one of the books exposing it is the *Holy Bible*. Jehovah encountered little resistance when he inflicted his mad scheme upon the Israeli people. As people are abducted in the twenty-first century, what evidence do we have that things will be any different if and when the aliens finally walk among us? The people who have been abducted – by their silence – actually become allies with our potential oppressors. The people who are abducted who feel they can't talk to anyone are, in their own strange way, helping the entities that are doing the abducting. Their silence enables the abductors to continue with their horrors.

This is a situation in which the aliens find that their cause is actually aided by what passes as human nature. The film *Fire in the Sky* was one of the rare films Hollywood has made to deal with alien abduction. It told the story of Travis Walton who was abducted for more than five days from the mountains of Arizona and was returned seven miles from his home. Those who saw the film did not see the full story. That was because the screenwriter (Tracy Torme) was pressured to come up with a different story regarding the abduction because it didn't satisfy the whims of the Hollywood investors. In their own strange way these investors were aiding the cause of the aliens. Sadly, making money pushed out the truth.

The only film that appeared to tell the truth about alien abductions was *The UFO Incident*, a film about the abduction of Betty and Barney Hill, a mixed-race couple, in New Hampshire back in 1961 (Betty was white, Barney was black). Both films dealt with the pain experienced during medical examinations. Both films dealt with the extreme fear that the abductees felt.

Another film that dealt with alien abductions was *Communion*, based on the best selling book by Whitley Strieber. In that film there is a scene of Whitley high-fiving the aliens – something that took away from the seriousness that the film was trying to explore. This couldn't help but support the alien cause.

Thus, aliens continue to abduct people with impunity. We seem to support their efforts by choosing to remain ignorant. Ignorance is bliss with so many people, yet few people are aware of their own ignorance. I now live in a retirement community where almost no one is aware of this problem.

Carl's Personal Experience with Alien Abduction

Carl is a gentleman in his early forties who has experienced alien abductions more than twenty times. He claims that he never knows when the experience will happen but when it does, it is quite unforgettable. Here he describes the latter part of his abduction experience:

> I am very uncomfortable with this situation. Quickly they move me into a "theater room" where they make me watch a video revealing how much we have polluted our environment. The video is highly upsetting; however, to be sure that we are watching, they clamp these metal attachments to my eyelids so that closing my eyes is impossible.
>
> Finally, I'm able to put my pajamas back on, and they take me back to my bedroom. It's freezing cold, and I'm worried about coming down with

something. When I'm back in bed, I find that I can't sleep. This is a problem that will go on for the next few weeks, and even then I don't sleep that well. As I'm lying in bed, I start thinking about who I can talk to about this and can't think of anyone. In the past I mentioned my experiences to a couple of my friends and discovered that they not only did not want to talk about this situation, but also no longer wanted to talk to me. I could tell by the looks I was getting from my therapist that she considered me to be a nut case.

The people who are abducted do not like being called "abductees." Instead they prefer to be called "experiencers." Cruel and unusual treatment is still cruel and unusual, even when you change the label. This is the way the aliens are treating us today – those they abduct, taking them against their will. What might they do when they no longer have to operate in secret? Evidently they are very fragile beings, physically, but have very large brain cases and can control us through mind power. They appear to be able to do what they want, and we evidently cannot do anything about it. What they may have in store for us may not be pretty.

Lori's Abduction Scenario

Most abduction scenarios have a common theme and a frightening consistency. This is not the case with "Lori." In so many ways her tale is more frightening than the "typical" abduction story.

Lori is a woman in her young 30's who chafes when she is called an *experiencer*. She insists, unlike most others, on being called an *abductee*. She understands that she is a victim and is not rationalizing the events into a happy little "experience."

[SPECIAL NOTE: Some of the language on the next few pages may be offensive to some people. However, I have chosen to leave it in because according to the victim, this was the exact language used when the incident originally happened.]

> My abduction began like so many abductions. I was sleeping when I woke and became aware of aliens being in my bedroom. They took me to a room that had only a few chairs. Seated in two of the chairs were two men in military uniforms. I was told to take off my clothes and I refused. At that point the two military men got up and wrestled me to the ground.
>
> 'Listen, you fucking cunt, you do exactly what these beings ask you to do!'

To drive home his point, one man doubled up his fist and smashed her in the face.

> I still resisted the aliens and the military men. I sat down with my back to all of them. It was only when the two military men held me down that they were able to undress me and allow the aliens to perform medical experiments on me. The two military men continued punching me,

and my body was racked with pain. The needles that they pushed into my stomach were not any fun either. But most of my pain came from the beatings I received from the military men.

"I actually saw one of the military men when I was in Santa Monica. He walked over to me and said, 'Just cooperate, just fucking cooperate.'"

If there is any chance that the aliens and the military are working together, this is an even greater horror story. The real horror lies in the average person's ignorance of what is really going on.

When I met Lori, I asked her, "Who is more cruel – the aliens of the humans?"

Without hesitation she answered, "The humans."

This is a horrifying enough; it's an even greater horror story if the military were responsible for the abduction, as some abductees have reported. If the aliens and military units are already working together in abduction scenarios, how much could we depend on our militaries to protect us, should the truth about their presence ever be made known?

A Most Horrifying Alien Abduction Account

The following story was related to me during a UFO convention by UFO researcher Derrel Sims, so I was unable to speak to the person involved first-hand. Nevertheless, I was told that during one of his investigations he came across a distraught woman who had experienced horrifying results related to alien abductions. Maureen had been abducted many times, but during her abductions she was not that cooperative. Finally, the aliens conveyed to her that if she didn't cooperate, they were going to bring tragedy into her life.

Evidently, these were aliens one doesn't mess with – she later came home one day to find her seventeen year-old son lying face down in their swimming pool, dead.

When she was abducted again the aliens made it clear that they were responsible and expected full cooperation from now on. Because she had other children, she decided to cooperate.

If the "gods" should ever return and we resist, how much of this behavior could we expect from them on a massive scale? If we are not going to plan for such events now, we should at least start thinking about how we could protect ourselves – especially if the military may end helping up helping those we would clearly oppose.

Chapter Five

A Possible Alien Horror: Cattle and Other Animal Mutilations

What Are Cattle Mutilations?

If there is one area where the aliens are playing dirty tricks, it lies in the area of cattle (and other animal) mutilations. First of all, few really know what cattle mutilations are, and even fewer care. For that reason alone, anything evil or negative that might come from the aliens is something we may have coming to us due to our ignorance. Hardly anyone knows or even cares about the problem. So what are cattle mutilations, and why should anyone care?

Jim Connors was riding his horse and surveying his ranch when he noticed something strange: two cattle were lying dead right in his path. He knew that cattle could be killed by predatory animals like coyotes and wolves. However, something was strange about these two dead cattle – something that he had never seen in his thirty-four years of ranching. The sex organs had been removed from both animals. One of the eyes and both of the ears were removed. What was strange was *how* the organs were removed. It appeared as if someone had removed these organs with the precision of a surgical scalpel. Alien implant removal surgeon Dr. Roger Leir would eventually come to the conclusion that these incisions had been done with a highly sophisticated laser-cutting instrument.

Then Connors noticed something very strange. While signs of predatory animals and swarms of maggots would normally be clearly evident, neither the predators nor the maggots would go anywhere near *these* dead animals. He did some quick calculating and determined that the loss of these two cattle would rob him of close to seven thousand dollars. Jim expected some losses because of predatory animals; however, this did not seem to fit and left him scratching his head in disbelief.

When Jim spoke about this with one of his neighbors, he was surprised by her response: "Just like me, it looks like you've had a cattle mutilation."

What happened to Jim and his neighbor was happening to many ranchers all across the western United States. When cattle die, a rancher usually calls upon a professional "remover" to get rid of the carcass. Jim found his conversation with this man interesting.

"This is the tenth one of these I've seen this year. I can't explain them. It's stranger than strange. We don't have anything that is sophisticated enough to do work like this. Whoever or whatever is doing this, is really messing with us."

UFO researcher Linda Moulton Howe has made an award-winning documentary about cattle mutilations called *Strange Harvest*.

In it, she has the doctors, researchers, and ranchers come forward and explain their own findings. As a result, one can see that a small group of people is taking this situation seriously. The main problem is that the news media aren't. That makes for a circumstance where the mass of humanity is kept in darkness. Those who research what people watch find that the average person is more interested in what is going on with Lindsay Lohan or reality TV than they are of being informed about serious problems facing humanity.

Thus, we end up getting what we want and will eventually end up getting what we deserve. Ignorance can have a devastatingly high cost. If the aliens are doing this, are we next? Are they just testing on the cattle before they move to the real targets?

Ranchers who experience cattle mutilations are very concerned. However, most other ranchers are not seriously interested – until they experience the same problem themselves.

Human Mutilations

This happening to cattle would be bad enough; however, the fact this might be happening to human beings is downright frightening. William English, who once worked with the CIA, tells the following story in a film I showed to one of my classes about a B-52 in Vietnam. It that had radioed in that it was under attack by a UFO and English was sent as part of a team to investigate.

> When I was stationed in Vietnam, our investigating unit was sent out to investigate a

plane crash. What we first noticed that was very strange was the fact that the plane was sitting on the ground fully intact. It was as if a giant hand had reached out and gently sat it down. There were no skid marks to indicate that the plane had actually crash landed. To get into the plane, we had to blow off the doors with explosives. Once we entered the plane, we were not prepared for what we saw. The pilot and passengers were all seated with their safety belts on, all looking eerily calm. We found that each one of them had had his sexual organs removed and that the left side of each person's face and the ears had been removed. This was a strange experience for all of us, and we were immediately sworn to secrecy. I am breaking my sworn oath by telling you about this today.

When I heard about this, I was driving on the Grapevine – a California freeway through the San Gabriel mountains on Interstate 5. It was late at night, and I was listening to a radio talk show. The Grapevine is an eerie place, and as I listened to William's account, I found myself feeling very strange. Since I was covering cattle mutilations in my critical thinking classes, I wondered if this interview was available on videotape. For years, I kept asking people at UFO conferences if they were aware of any such tape. Finally, I encountered Lazlo, a Hungarian UFO researcher, who said he had a videotape of William English that he had purchased in Hungary. He eventually made a copy and sent it to me.

There, after a year and a half of searching, I finally had my video, and there was William describing the incident I have just related.

I showed the tape to my critical thinking classes; the comment from one of my students sums up the impact it made on them:

"Thanks for ruining my day."

Other Animal Mutilations

If the problem of cattle mutilations doesn't generate enough concern, consider the situation of Linda.

Linda, after a busy day of teaching kindergarten, came home and expected her dog to come running up to her as it always had. When Linda went through the house and into the fenced back yard, she saw something very upsetting. There, on the ground, was her three-year-old dog, lying on its back with its sexual organs removed. A closer examination revealed that one of its eyes was missing. Also, parts of the face were scraped away. She immediately called her veterinarian.

Linda thought the vet would be shocked, and was shocked herself that she wasn't.

"This is the third one of these I have seen," the vet said. "Other vets have seen the same thing. One has actually seen five examples of this."

Evidently, whoever or whatever is doing this has not singled out simply ranchers with cattle. The targeting of people's pets is sad and shocking. The mutilators' concern for human feelings is apparently non-existent. Some UFO researchers claim that the military is conducting clandestine experiments. Other researchers claim it's the aliens. Whether earthbound or alien, the lack of respect is legion. For animal pets, one does not have the economic damage; however, the emotional damage can be severe. If you presently own a pet or have previously owned one, imagine what you would feel if you experienced the same situation.

It is not just dogs that are being mutilated; cats have also experienced mutilation. One farmer even woke to find his goat had suffered the same fate.

The fact is that the average person has not directly experienced any kind of animal mutilation. The person says to himself, "If it has not happened to me, it does not exist." The person goes through a subconscious process of declaring it "irrelevant." Therefore, no help is coming for those personally affected. Once again, if the aliens – or our military – are involved, then they are winning.

Hundreds of ranchers have been affected by cattle mutilations. This should give one pause; however, it rarely does. This is a serious problem with much deeper implications that seen on the surface. Yet few care because in most cases, there is nothing that directly affects the average person. At a later time, however, that could change.

Who is doing all the mutilating of farm animals? The aliens, most likely. Some researchers speculate that the mutilation phenomenon may be part of a secret military operation. Yet, what on earth could dead animals have to do with the military? It doesn't make any sense.

Some aliens, who have directly contacted humans, have claimed no responsibility and have said that as far as mutilations go, that we are on our own – in effect, pointing the finger at the military.

Who do we believe? Who is actually responsible? Whoever is doing it remains unknown to this day – whether alien forces or secret military forces. The fact that the technology used is superior to anything known to medical practitioners today could present an opportunity for the human race in general. Laser surgery is a relatively new discovery for us, but has been an integral part of cattle mutilations from the beginning. Medical laser cutting units are huge and cumbersome, and could never have been taken out into the field as portable devices when these mutilations were happening.

Although ranchers, pet owners and of course the animal victims are the only ones directly affected, those who have done this leave no doubt that some kind of advanced technology is involved. As part of the larger mosaic, these mutilations go a long way toward pointing out that we might not be alone.

Note: For the above chapter I owe a great debt to Tony Presser, who provided a good portion of the research.

Chapter Six

Crop Circles

One of the areas that might be closely related to work done by the aliens is crop circles. Crop circles are large formations that appear overnight in farmers' fields, mainly in England. The patterns are very intricate, can be seen much better from the air, and many of them are quite beautiful.

I first learned about crop circles in the summer of 1991 during the annual MUFON (Mutual UFO Network) convention in Chicago. There, crop circle expert Colin Andrews spoke to an astonished audience about the phenomenon. He even showed a daytime video of a small UFO flying over one crop circle. At the time, he was convinced that these phenomena were the result of alien intervention. Now he has stunned audiences by claiming that 80% of crop circles are done by the British military.

If this is the case, what about the other twenty percent? But more importantly, why would the British military go to the trouble and enormous expense of creating hundreds of crop circles? That doesn't make any sense.

Here we have an amazingly confusing situation. Andrews claims that he cannot explain 20% of these formations, but he is positive that 80% of them are done by the British military.

Crop formation experts call themselves "cereologists" and claim to be able to tell the real circles from the fake ones. In real ones, they say, the crops are only bent, not broken.

Among the ranks of the cereologists, the most fervent is Michael Glickman. He protested vigorously when Colin Andrews declared that 80% of them were fakes produced by the military. An inventor, architect and engineer who has been employed as a professor at respected universities, Glickman gushes almost poetically about the mystic beauty of the crop circles. To him, there is a profound mathematical beauty inherent in their designs, which can only be unearthly in origin. One of the most complex formations was of a Mandelbrot set.

The Mandelbrot set is a particular mathematical set of points, whose boundary generates a distinctive and easily recognizable two-dimensional fractal shape. The set is closely related to the Julia set (which generates similarly complex shapes), and is named after the mathematician Benoît Mandelbrot, who studied and popularized it. Three days before the Mandelbrot Set was actually discovered by mathematicians, the perfect set appeared in a field in England. No one can explain that. It just happened.

As one researcher remarked, "Someone or something is messing with us."

On September 9, 1991, the British tabloid *Today* ran a front-page story headlined: "The Men Who Conned The World." The story claimed that all the crop circles in England were the work of two retired pensioners, 67-year-old Doug Bower and 62-year-old David Chorley. Their tools were basically a four-foot plank of wood and a ball of string, along with a piece of wire dangling from a baseball cap to serve as a sighting device, enabling them to construct perfectly straight lines by focusing on a distant object – in almost total darkness!

To flatten the stalks of grain in areas that did not overlap the tramlines made by tractors when spraying crops, they said they had stood inside a tramline and then jumped or pole-vaulted into the grain field. This would have required two senior citizens to pole-vault up to 35 feet – which would have, at the very least, qualified them for a silver medal in the Olympics. They said that the idea of making crop circles had come to them after a boring evening at a pub in 1978, and their only motive was to 'have a laugh." Not only had they never been seen doing this, their wives had never noticed them being gone at night.

A couple of days after this story appeared in the British tabloid, it hit the global news wires. In the US, on NBC Nightly News, Tom Brokaw – in fourteen seconds of airtime – announced that crop circles were now fully explained as hoaxes. Every news medium in the country, broadcast and print, repeated the same story on the same day. Of questions about the veracity of this fantastic tale, there were none. No news outlet evinced skepticism, no reporter investigated this claim – they simply repeated it.

Case closed.

The problem is that one of the men died – and the patterns increased and became more intricate. The NBC Brokaw farce put many minds at ease, but its information was far from a rational explanation of the problem. People with limited world-views need quick and easy answers to explain away their problems. Many people just can't stand to admit there are mysteries in the world that we currently do not know about. It's too uncomfortable for them, so the news media are more than happy to step in and accommodate them by explaining away their fears and concerns.

For another example, at a time when people did not know the cause of AIDS, Pastor Jerry Falwell saw the AIDS epidemic of the 1980's as nothing more than God's punishment being heaped upon gay people for their "sins." No scientific or medical explanation was necessary because his followers wanted to believe it.

In the area of religion, seventy million people in America have no problem thinking that all their "sins" will be forgiven if they only accept Jesus Christ as their personal savior. All the Islamic students I had at College of Sequoias firmly believed that the Earth was only 6,000 years old. Their reason: that is what Mohammed stated in the *Koran*. Scientific evidence was irrelevant to these students. In fact, they claimed the devil put out this false information.

The crop circle phenomenon is apparently so threatening that most people actually blot it out from their perception. That is the easy thing to do.

However, the problem with easy answers is that they are not always *good* answers. When I was in seminary studying to be a minister of the Gospel, I remember one heated discussion. We couldn't agree which of the theologians we were studying were in heaven or in hell. Carl Barth was, by almost unanimous decision, in hell. (You must remember that I was enrolled in a fundamentalist seminary – and at the time bought into what they were teaching.) Paul Tillich was evenly divided between heaven and hell. C.S. Lewis was definitely in heaven.

The same situation crops up (pardon the pun) at UFO conventions. A majority believes crop circles are the result of alien technology. However, a significant plurality doesn't know what to believe. In this circumstance, it is actually easier to believe the alien intervention hypothesis, because the phenomena are actually very mysterious. Most people simply avoid thinking about it.

That unfortunately doesn't stop crop circles from manifesting. In fact, they are now appearing in other countries – like Russia, Brazil, and the United States. Now one need not fly to England in order to see crop circles. Furthermore, crop formations are not simply a recent phenomenon. In his article "Crop Circles and Their Message," author David Pratt reveals the following:

> In 1686 a British scientist, Robert Plot, published a book entitled *A Natural History of Staffordshire*, which contained accounts of geometric areas of flattened plants found on both arable land and pastureland. He describes not only circles but also spirals and squares within rings, up to 150 feet across. He reports that the

soil under them was much looser and drier than normal, and that a whitish, musty substance or hoar, "like that in moldy bread," was sometimes found on the plants.

He hypothesized that lightning exploding from the clouds created the designs. In July, 1880 the science journal *Nature* published a letter from a scientist who described finding multiple circular areas of flattened wheat on a farm in southern England.

He suggested they were the result of "some cyclonic wind action."

While I have been to South America (mainly Peru and Argentina) and spent two separate months in France researching the Knights Templar, I have not specifically taken a flight to England to observe the crop circles. Therefore, I have not experienced this phenomenon up close and personal. My interest in crop circles is purely intellectual – without the kind of visceral involvement of a Colin Andrews or Michael Glickman.

Crop circles would not appear to be a negative problem like alien abductions or cattle mutilations; however, one only needs to see this from the viewpoint of the farmer of the wheat or rape fields. Curious people come to these farms and trample through the crops. Many farmers put up donation boxes requesting help to cover their costs, and for the most part people are generous and help the farmers recover at least a portion of their lost income. Yet, as beautiful as these formations can be, farmers are most often not able to recover the cost of the damaged crops. Some farmers, as a result, destroy these beautiful creations as soon as they see them.

Whatever these crop formations are, from a practical and purely mundane standpoint, they amount to cosmic vandalism or extraterrestrial graffiti. It makes one wonder if a group of extraterrestrial juvenile delinquents (or perhaps "senior citizens" – not of the Earth like Doug and Dave, but of the galaxy) are "having a laugh" at our expense. However, if this phenomenon has a deeper and more profound explanation, no one has yet determined it.

There are some researchers who have in fact claimed to decode messages in these elaborate formations from a much higher, quite likely, off-planet intelligence. Yet, the proof is not entirely clear in these situations. Symbols like this are open to many different interpretations. For now, their meanings remain up to the believer – but at some point, if the "gods" do return, maybe the meaning of the crop circles will be explained to us then.

Many of these circles are quite elaborate and incredibly beautiful. People from all over the world come to England to observe them. Something intelligent is making them and they are definitely not made entirely by good ol' boys like Doug and Dave. Is it the aliens? That seems to be a likely explanation. Crop circles by themselves are not enough to prove the existence of an alien presence on planet Earth. But they provide tantalizing clues. Although they remain a mystery, they represent a stone sober reality: whoever is creating them is far superior to us in physics, math and technology. Whoever has such technology has a plethora of gifts to offer the human race. However, the human race may not be ready for them – particularly because most of us don't care.

If we were serious about other forms of intelligent life, we would put major media focus on the crop circles and put our best scientists at work on cracking their code. Until such time, we may be deemed unworthy and too ignorant to develop any communication with whomever is responsible.

Chapter Seven

The Miracle of Fatima
The Aliens' 20th Century Grand Deception

The aliens might intentionally be trying to deceive us. For those willing to explore this issue, we humans just might be the victims of an elaborate deception program and sometimes, an occasional practical joke. I experienced this when I went out to the Laguna Mountains and encountered a UFO that defied logic by making extremely unusual noises. One can possibly see this in the phenomenon of crop circles and even more with the incidents of cattle mutilations. However it is the area of alien abductions where the agenda of the aliens is seen as a greater horror. This can also be seen with the virgin Mary appearances which happened in 1917, with similar visitations currently happening all over the world.

The most famous of these was the appearance in Fatima, Portugal in 1916 and 1917. There, three children (Lucia. Jacinta, and Francisco) witnessed the appearance of "a most beautiful woman" who spoke to them. She told them that mankind must turn from their sinful ways. World War I was still raging in Europe. She gave the children three distinct messages that were meant for the pope.

During her first appearance, the "beautiful woman" admonished the children for their lack of faith and suggested to them that they say the rosary every day. Here, we have a demand that the children continue their slave chip conditioning by the use of repetition. Because this was done under the guise of a miracle, the children had no choice but to obey.

During the second apparition, Mary made it plain that men and women were basically sinners and needed to convert to the Catholic faith. This, like incidents from ancient history, are shown to be tactics of control and conditioning. During the period following this apparition all three children were accused of lying by the townspeople. Some priests then suggested that the entity appearing to the children was actually the devil. Jacinta was so convinced of this that she at first refused to go to the next apparition. In the second apparition, emphasis was placed on the sinful nature of humans and all were admonished to say the rosary every day. This is like some of the more modern space brothers' channeling – stating that humans are depraved and need to turn their lives around.

During the third apparition Mother Mary upped the ante. She showed Lucia a vision of hell that she (Lucia) claimed years later was one of the most terrifying experiences of her life. She also claimed that the war was going to go on, and that Russia needed to be converted to the Catholic faith. "Mary" also gave Lucia some devastating news: her closest friends, Jacinta and Francisco, would die very soon. When Lucia began crying and stated that she would be all alone, "Mary" attempted to comfort her by stating that she ("Mary") would always be with her (aside from a couple of perfunctory personal appearances,

Lucia was in fact left alone.) Some comfort. When Lucia asked about friends of hers, she was assured that most were in heaven and that one was in purgatory. Purgatory is an area of purging in which the Catholic Church is attempting to ignore or distance itself from. However this was 1917 and the concern about Purgatory was something to be taken seriously.

"Mary" evidently had the power to extend the lives of Francisco and Jacinto, but this was not one of her priorities. She also had the option to show Lucia visions of a world at peace or visions of heaven; however she chose to portray the horrors of hell and sinners writhing in agony instead. Lucia was a very young child (ten years old), and "Mary" evidently knew that this would be a horrifying experience for Lucia.

"Mary" also told the three children that they could contribute to keeping sinners out of hell if they would personally make sacrifices. It was hot during the summer of 1917 and the children began their sacrifices by lying flat on the ground and refusing to drink water as long as they could endure it. Each of them was severely dehydrated. However, they continued the sacrifice by abstaining from food until they finally had to eat. "Mary" assured them on their next meeting that their sacrifices had indeed kept many sinners from facing the torments of hell. The theory here is that sinners deserve hell, yet they can be rescued from this horrid fate by the sacrifices of others. The idea of sacrifice is an Old Testament concept that was inflicted many times upon the emerging human race by the ancient aliens. It is no surprise that the aliens would want to keep this concept alive; however, they dressed it up by aligning it with noble actions.

I firmly believe that the Fatima incident was brought about by the aliens in order to insure their control of humans. When reading what follows in the sixth apparition, one is more willing to accept this idea.

The fourth and fifth apparitions were fairly uneventful except for the fact that "Mary" indicated to the children that they needed to come back the following month on the thirteenth and that all of them – despite the fact that two of them would die young – should say the rosary every day as long as they lived. However it was during this period that Lucia asked "Mary" to provide a miracle so that more believers would be brought into the fold. This "Mary" promised to do it, and it turned out to be a whopper.

When the children asked for a sign so that they could help others believe, "Mary," during her sixth appearance, allegedly had the sun twirl down in a spinning circle, and dry up the rain-soaked people. To show what the aliens had as their priority, "Mary's" agenda was to deepen belief in the Catholic religion. "Mary" made it very clear to Lucia that she had to say the rosary every day, and that sinners had to convert to the Catholic religion. Otherwise, they would languish in hell.

In Fatima, she appeared on the thirteenth of each month for five straight months.

UFO experts and Catholic Church leaders each have their own theories about the Fatima event. I lean more toward the UFO people and think that the aliens created the "event." First of all, the sun cannot careen toward the earth. The sun was not its normal color during this event and had more of a silvery appearance. In addition, I have personally seen spiraling UFOs descend from the sky. The fact that the rain-soaked people ended up completely dry, could be explained by heat coming from the UFO. The children asked for a discernable sign and they received it.

This book's mission is to point out how the aliens could well be carrying on their grand deception up through our modern times. Fellow critical thinking teacher Tony Presser and I traveled to Southern California a few years ago to check out a phenomenon know simply as the Mother Mary Apparitions. On the 13th of each month hundreds – and sometimes as many as five thousand – people would gather at this place referred to as the Rock of Mary. On this day Mary would appear to a channeler and give a message for mankind.

This would happen each month (on the thirteenth!) and be preceded by appearances in the sky. This location and its continuing events is the most recent of what is known today as Marian appearances.

Tony and I traveled to this spot – and around 11:00 a.m. people began gasping and pointing towards the sky. A woman, who happened to be the only other non-Hispanic American at the scene, pointed at the sky and said to us: "Do you see it?"

Both of us claimed that we could not see anything. She then pointed her Polaroid camera toward the same direction that she had been pointing. The pictures that came out showed there was something very bright up in the clouds. Tony and I were the equivalent of the Patagonian natives when they first encountered the ships of Magellan. This is a well-documented story. When the natives at the Patagonian Islands encountered the explorer Magellan's boats, they could see the smaller ones that brought his men into shore; however, they could not see their big boat – despite it being in plain sight. This is because they had never seen anything like it before, so it did not fit into any pre-existing concept that would allow them to recognize it. Eventually the shamans (holy men, medicine men) could see fuzzy images of the boat, but only after shifting their consciousness. Once the shamans described what was out there, the natives began to see it.

After seeing the Polaroid photos of the lights in the sky, I felt like one of those natives during this visit to the Rock of Mary. Of the five hundred present, 90% were most likely from Mexico, quite likely on a pilgrimage. One of the women who spoke broken English tried to fill us in as to what the woman channeling Mary was saying. This woman who translated for us had a dedication and passion that I have seen in few human beings. She felt it was essential that we get the message of "Mary" and, though she struggled mightily with her English, did not give up on us. Her passion and concern for the two of us touched us deeply.

In broken English she translated the woman who was channeling "Mary." She told us, "She claims that bad times will be upon us shortly. To atone for our sins, we must build a church and an orphanage on this spot."

However, why would the aliens do such a thing? The pronouncement that a church and orphanage be built is something that would have played well a century ago. However, the idea of an orphanage in modern America is absurd. The aliens might just have to change their message in order to maintain their credibility. It seems clear they are continuing in their devious ways, and enjoy messing with humanity.

The 1917 Fatima event still maintains an interest with programs on the History Channel, National Geographic Channel and others. The three messages that the children received still fascinate people today – although the final message is more confusing than clear. Some claim to know the third message and, despite different versions, try to influence human thought by giving an interpretation.

The "mission" of the aliens is to and always has been to deceive, exploit and confuse. If ever they have "helped" us, it has been more for their own benefit. With the Fatima event and the monthly Marian appearances in California, they just might be achieving these objectives.

To our credit, the last I knew, no one was doing anything about building a church and an orphanage twenty miles from the nearest town – well outside of the bigger towns of Lancaster and Palmdale, California. Meanwhile, Tony and I left scratching our heads, feeling like Patagonian natives and wondering why we failed to see the lights in the sky.

Chapter Eight

The Ancient Aliens' Devastating Conditioning
The Slave Chip

What Is the Slave Chip?

The slave chip is not anything new. It was "implanted" in humanity thousands of years ago. We, as newly created humans, were not a blessing to our masters. We complained loudly about how brutal and dirty the work was. The aliens eventually gave us a conditioning so strong that we are still dominated by it today. When I say they were our creators, allow me to clarify. We already existed when the aliens arrived, but in a more primitive form. They "created" us by tampering with our genetics. The idea was to fashion a more intelligent being that would be smart enough to do the work they required, but stupid enough not to rebel. When they finally perfected the right genetic combination, *we* were the result – with the "slave chip" as part of genetic make-up.

The slave chip is like a computer program. Once placed in us, the same results can be expected continuously. The program is not a helpful one for us, but then that was not the aliens' – our creators' – intention. The intention was that we consider ourselves slaves and workers for the gods. The idea was that we would worship them, venerate them and, most importantly, obey them.

The genetic alterations were not totally effective in the beginning. The newly created humans did not respond well to authority (see the *Popul Vuh* quotes in chapter three). Therefore, a new wrinkle in the genetic code was introduced, which made us bend more easily to the will of authorities. To take full advantage of this, these aliens insisted that they were God Almighty, and it somehow became "holy" for us to bend to God's will. Religion was born.

The slave chip is so powerful that it works in both individual and collective ways. While one, through effort, can break free of the *individual* programming, it is more difficult for humans as a group to dent the collective slave chip. Those who effectively urge others to break free and get beyond their slave conditioning, tend to get marginalized, sneered at, attacked, or even assassinated. History bears this out. Gandhi, Martin Luther King, Jr. and many others paid with their lives for freeing people from the slave chip mentality. The programming of the slave chip has resulted in strong cultural conditioning that can reinforce our fear against doing anything about it – even after we find out that it's there.

The slave chip's collective programming helps humans see a limiting life as noble, and a life with freedom as irresponsible. These modes of thinking are very powerful and never based on original thought. Instead, what comes from the slave chip may be embraced as "the right way to act" in a social context, or "the Truth" in a religious one. Working hard and taking orders instead of working smart and being creative is seen as the "way to go." No original thought is found here. With the slave chip, giving up something valuable in order to get something that allows only for your basic existence can be seen as realistic and practical.

I am a retired college teacher. Were it not for the programming of the slave chip, few people would go to college. The idea of students sitting in a classroom absorbing "knowledge" from a teacher standing in front of the room when they might get far superior knowledge from personal experience, traveling abroad or surfing the Internet with research skills is absurd. Thanks to my own slave chip conditioning, I had a steady job for almost forty years. Nevertheless, I was aware of the chip and its impact – on myself and my students. I would sometimes say to my students, "Get the hell out of here. Go see the world. It might not be a friendly place, but it can teach you a lot more than I can."

Of course, in most cases I only received looks of disbelief. Students wondered why I would debase myself as a teacher – but I was teaching them in a new and different way that could cause a positive change. Some of them "got it," and experienced such amazing results that I still hear from them to this day. Causing a huge positive shift in a student's life is a gratifying experience.

I would not have had the privilege of doing that, while at the same time making a decent wage doing something that I loved, if I had not been bored to tears listening to traditional lectures about the Boston Latin schools and teaching methods. If I had not been skeptical of the traditional teaching paradigm, I could have never become a "real" teacher. At the beginning of my career, I taught unsuspecting high school students whom I had the "privilege" of boring into academic submission. It brought back memories of my own years as a student, listening to boring, traditional teachers. Then, for a while, I became one.

During practice teaching, I had a master teacher named Jim Bowers who sat at the back of the room and observed me. He must have been bored out of his mind. I became a professional master teacher myself and was in charge of prospective teachers at Eastern Michigan University. I only survived that job for a year, because I started to teach students differently. Those who question the value of a college education are considered to be "out of touch with reality." Although I had not yet named it, I had identified the slave chip and was trying to deprogram it from my students while still maintaining my job. I became successful at this for many years. Now that I am retired, it is time to spread these teachings outside of college classrooms.

How the Slave Chip Works

The slave chip is extremely powerful. How can one defeat it? One cannot overcome the effects of the slave ship by the New Age method of writing affirmations over and over. This has been tried without success many times. The slave chip is deeply rooted and will not "go gently into the night." First of all, one needs to learn how the slave chip works.

The programming and conditioning we receive from the slave chip are powerful. They can cause us to choose experiences that limit rather than fulfill us. This conditioning will cause us to settle for a career based on what others think rather than choosing a meaningful vocation for yourself. It can also cause a person to choose work based on how much money she can make instead of doing what she loves to do. Seeking fulfillment is not in the programming of the slave chip. Personal fulfillment gets sacrificed. How interesting that the word "sacrifice" comes from the Latin roots *"sacra"* and *"fice"* – meaning "to make sacred." The aliens gave us a conditioning so strong that we, as modern humans, have a hard time getting over it.

The slave chip really is like a modern computer program, installed in human DNA rather than silicon. Once bred into us, it runs automatically and continuously. The program is not a happiness-inducing program – but that was not the intention of our "creators." The ancient aliens wanted us to consider ourselves as slaves, obedient workers for the gods ("to worship" and "to work for" come from the same Sumerian root word). They ultimately wanted us to idolize and revere them as our spiritual leaders.

The aliens did this by convincing humans that there was only one true GOD, and they were IT. In fact, they were HIM. There were two major elements to the religion they created for us: monotheism and patriarchy. This required demonizing (literally) every other putative deity the human race had been worshiping, and by demoting females to an inferior status.

Even now, thousands of years later, some people can only relate to a God who is male. My good friend Jane Thompson, who is a pastor's wife, would upset people when she constantly referred to God as "she." Even during the "Apostles' Creed" Jane would say, "She will come to judge the quick and the dead." This evidently was not within the paradigm of being a good pastor's wife and probably contributed to her husband Don being removed from their present church. Jane was not a paragon of a minister's wife.

The slave chip helps to create inner conflict when you are trying to decide what is best for you, or trying to decide what to do about something. For example, suppose you decide one day to give up your job as a bank loan officer or whatever job you have, and spend your time whittling whales and porpoises out of driftwood that you find on the beach, and selling them. Although you are only thinking about it, you can expect your mind to serve up the following thoughts:

"You want to do *what!*"

"That's selfish and immature."

"What are you... freaking crazy?"

"Face reality, and stop being stupid."

"Jobs are hard work. You can't make a living from something you love."

"If you keep this up, your soul is in danger."

The last example shows up in organized religion. The sad irony here is that the soul is most likely *urging* you to break free. When I was in seminary studying to be a pastor, I would ask questions that would make my fellow students uncomfortable.

My professor, Dr. Roger Nicole, would often quip, "Mr. Barranger, you are quickly walking away from the footsteps of Jesus."

When I would attempt to sit in the cafeteria with other students, some of them would say, "Jack, please sit somewhere else – I can't take you today."

During a visit from the well-known evangelical apologist John Montgomery, Professor Nicole actually apologized for questions I was asking. John Montgomery replied, "If he can't ask these questions here, where else *can* he ask them?" It was great to hear that.

The slave chip was honed to perfection thousands of years ago. Only now are we becoming aware of how it is impacting human society and how monumental the problem is.

The Slave Chip in Modern Society

Certain societies are in no way evil; but that is contrary to what most are conditioned to believe.

I learned this when, during the mid 1960's, I visited what at that time was East Germany. I had been conditioned by my society to believe that because that country was communist, all of the people were slaves, and I did not expect the people to be friendly. I was lost when I got off the train at the wrong stop and somehow had to make my way from East Berlin to West Berlin. I was shaking in my boots – surely I was going to be thrown in jail. I approached an East German border guard and told him my situation. He was gentle and understanding. (Thank God I spoke German fairly well.) He claimed that lots of people end up in that situation, and he walked with me to the entrance to West Berlin. The West German border guard told me that many people made it to freedom because the East German guards, when shooting, intentionally missed their targets. I found East Germans who loved their children and had dreams like mine. When I was lost and looked lost, people walked up to me and asked if they could help.

America is a country where the conditioning about God is fairly strong. "God" help any political candidate who doesn't believe in God. We are the only country where the idea of prayer in schools can push a few hot buttons. The idea of free will is given lip service; however, anyone genuinely expressing free will outside of the socially accepted paradigm may endure the wrath of the self-righteous. It reminds me of a saying we had in the 1960's: The only thing a non-conformist hates worse than a conformist is another nonconformist who won't conform to the prevailing standards of non-conformity.

Self-righteous people want to see more restrictions on what others say and do. Take, for instance, Hollywood movies. Those who control movie content in Hollywood have little problem with violence, but sex is taboo. Although I can no longer recall who it was, one famous movie star once said:

> If you bite off a woman's breast, that will get you a PG rating; however, if you kiss the breast, that will get you an NC-17 rating.

Compare that to the more open European approach to sex and you can see societal conditioning at work.

What does this have to do with the slave chip? One grows up with ones' societal conditioning, and ones' cultural mores are affected by that conditioning. When I taught in Denmark for a year, I experienced cultural shock with the Danes' "non-guilt" approach to sex. I did not see the Danes flagrantly espousing sex; they just accepted it as an ordinary part of human nature, and I eventually found their attitude most refreshing.

American attitudes toward work are influenced by the slave chip. The Puritan Work Ethic runs a strong program in the United States. People are not exactly inspired to seek work that is satisfying as much as they are "driven" to seek work that is prestigious. My father constantly harassed me to go into a "man's profession" instead of becoming a teacher. He continued his harassment until he read letters my students wrote to me when I was in Denmark.

That year in Denmark helped me move closer to a shift that eventually caused my release from the slave chip's conditioning. One of my previous books, *Freedom From Religion*, originally began with the title of *Deprogramming the Slave Chip*. It is meant to help others break free of the slave chip's devastating programming – mostly in regard to religion (therefore the title change). I have now revived *Deprogramming the Slave Chip*, a book meant to help others break free in all areas of life.

Chapter Nine

Concerns and Conclusions

Are the "gods" coming back soon? Or are they already here? The subject is akin to the potential dangers of global warming. Some believe it – some do not. The vast majority of people think the idea that aliens are here is ridiculous. But what if they are? Upon researching the subject closely, it seems that *something* is going on, and it should not be swept under the rug. Much like global warming, it is a good idea not to ignore it because if it is true, we'd better prepare ourselves (just in case).

I have presented evidence that aliens, who called themselves "gods," were here in the ancient past and are visiting planet Earth today. For me personally, I'm fairly convinced they are here today. The one thing that will make me certain is when they openly announce themselves. I talked to many people who believe they have encountered aliens. They are firmly convinced that the aliens are here and that they present a problem for mankind. I became a "near believer" when I interviewed the more than forty men and women who claimed to be abducted by aliens. The more I learned about cattle and other animal mutilations the more of a believer I became. However, during research for my book *Past Shock*, I became even more convinced that aliens had visited us in our ancient past.

I am a seminary graduate. If I wanted, I could pastor a church. (That would be my view of hell on Earth.) However, I have strong doubts about the existence of God due, in part, to uncovering the truth about those who masqueraded as gods and bestowed upon us the "slave chip." I don't find that worth worshipping. That could be a major roadblock to any effective pastoring.

Mother Teresa (for different reasons) experienced the same feelings close to her passing. My dear friend Bill claims that God can handle my doubt; I tell him that I don't believe there is a God to handle my doubt. He once sent me the manuscript of a book he had written called *Liberating Truths*, which was so full of God images that I was offended. He, like so many people who are part of the innocuous New Age movement and strongly believe in aliens, look forward to their coming. Ironically, he is the one who gave me John Lear's "run like hell" quote – which was Lear's advice on what to do when seeing a UFO.

A trusted friend claims to have seen a gray alien in his motel room at Nevada's famous Area 51 shortly after having an amazing sighting of five craft that same night in the desert. At Area 51, I and a fellow English teacher from College of the Sequoias encountered so many lights in the sky that on that evening we were nudged closer to believing in aliens ourselves. What kept our doubts alive is the fact that Area 51 is a military base that has a history of secret test flights for advanced planes like Stealth bombers. Out near Area 51 we met three students from San Diego State who had no problem believing in the reality of aliens.

Concerns and Conclusions 95

Those who have had experiences with aliens tend to want additional proof to validate their experience. They, like most alien abductees, choose to attend UFO conferences in an effort to seek this proof. An encounter with aliens is so incredibly bizarre and most often unexpected, so it comes as a shock to these people. They often need help in coming to grips with these experiences. Their operating paradigm never included the idea of aliens, so trying to make room for the idea, especially after strange encounters like these, is a huge challenge. This reminds me of the great German philosopher Hegel, who said, " With accuracy only, you can never reach the truth." Truth is often never found with what we know – no matter how accurate it might seem to be. We must learn to look in new ways or, by doing so, to interpret things in new ways. We are creatures of habit, so existing paradigms tend to limit our beliefs rather than enhance them. New forms of sensory input are also quite shocking and are often experienced in these encounters. Our habitual, day-to-day paradigm is not friendly toward new forms of sensory input – it can be overwhelming, which is sometimes found with these people.

As mentioned earlier, when the Patagonian natives witnessed Magellan's arrival, they could see the smaller boats that brought his men to shore, but could not see their big boat until the shamans, with more powerful minds, finally did so and pointed them out to the others. When I gave this historically documented example in one of my critical thinking classes, a woman came up to me and informed me that she was going to drop the class because she couldn't believe what she was hearing. She was an example of a person with a severely limited paradigm.

Most of us in society have limited paradigms. When it comes to aliens being on planet Earth, we might be failing to see the big boat. What causes us to not see "the big boat" in all areas of life? I believe it comes from the slave chip. In general, we've been programmed to accept only what we know and believe without examining other possibilities. There's a hidden script, or tape loop, that continually plays in the background of our subconscious minds that says, "The only way I can maintain my beliefs is by never examining them." There are many other similar scripts, but this is the one that keeps us from seeing "the big ships."

One of my students who had seen the William English B-52 human mutilation film (mentioned earlier) said she wanted to come in next semester when I showed that segment again.

"I want to see the look on your student's faces," she said.

"I think you will learn more about paradigms, than you will learn about aliens," I said.

Many potential students refused to take my classes because they heard I believed in UFOs. Literally speaking, I had seen "the big ships." (When you have multiple UFO sightings, you tend to become a believer.) Others would drop my critical thinking class because the subject of inductive reasoning dealt with the issue of cattle mutilations. I had in my textbook pictures of mutilated cows, and this proved to be too much for a number of students. One student stormed out of class with the following pronouncement:

"One thing your class has convinced me is that I need to read my Bible more!"

How interesting that most people can read their Bibles and not see where it talks about alien intervention. In Genesis Chapter Six the word "Nefilim" is used. The word Nefilim really means "those who from the sky came." But in the Bible the word is translated as "giants." That's a good safe word. That would not upset too many people.

When the prophet Ezekiel saw a large "chariot" coming down from the sky, he was describing it from his own limited paradigm. He could not describe it as an "alien spacecraft" because his limited paradigm had only "chariots" as the nearest thing he could use to describe it.

These things are described not only in the Bible, but throughout history. Even Alexander the Great and his soldiers saw strange lights in the sky, and what they experienced the most – because of their limited knowledge – was fear.

We must open ourselves up to the possibility of their return. If we continue to have limited paradigms, we are setting ourselves up for potential danger. The aliens are counting on humanity to have these limited paradigms so they won't be discovered. They programmed us this way – to put our beliefs over factual evidence. This is part of the slave chip. What they may have planned for us, based on their own past actions, may not be pretty. Like in the past, they may expect to be worshiped when they return. We offered little resistance in ancient times. Our religions have been conditioning us to one day blindly accept, once again, any entity that is technologically superior and see them as gods. However, we can be sure of one thing: any resistance will be met with severe penalties. History is not something to be merely studied as just stories from the dusty past; it is prologue to what we can expect once the aliens reveal themselves.

In journeying through this book you have discovered that all was not love and light with the aliens. They were technologically superior as seen by edifices in Baalbek, Egypt, Peru and many other places worldwide. I have personally been to Egypt and Peru and have experienced the wonders of the pyramids and the technologically advanced stone structures of Cuzco. One could not see Baalbek at the time I wished to go, because it was a volatile military area at the time and Lebanon would not allow it but, as I understand, people may now visit this incredible place. It contains the largest stone blocks in the world – blocks so large that the largest modern cranes would have immense trouble lifting them, much less move them any distance whatsoever. The huge stone blocks of the Great Pyramid in Egypt also remain a mystery as to how such massive stone could be moved to such a great height without any means to do so that would make any sense. Other than we had help.

While these visiting "gods" were highly advanced technologically, they were sadly lacking in spiritual matters. In this area they have little to offer us. In matters regarding spiritual advancement, we are better than they are. We could learn from them in matters technological; they can learn from us in matters spiritual. When they return one day, we should make every effort to avoid their exploitation and manipulation from a religious and spiritual standpoint.

When I was at the alien technology conference and experienced that devastating conversation with five other people and told them if the aliens came back, I was going to hide in a cave, they looked at me as if I were the most spiritually arrogant person they had ever seen.

If what I have written shows spiritual arrogance, so be it.

Appendix A

Why I Believe that the Aliens are Here

The aliens are nowhere.

The aliens are now here.

Which of the above statements reflects for you the truth about planet Earth? Both have the exact same letters; however, both reflect different world views. Let's try again.

The "aliens" will be "landing" soon.

The aliens will be landing soon.

The first sentence is very safe. It allows us to make that statement without sounding crazy; the second sentence is more alarming because it requires more commitment on the part of the speaker/writer. Yet both contain the exact same letters.

This Appendix is for those who wish to read about some of my evidence. If you already believe the aliens are here, then you may not need to be convinced by my words, but reading this could still provide some confirmation for you. If you don't believe in alien beings you may still want to amuse yourself by reading about some experiences the author is completely convinced that he has had with UFOs. If your belief is in a gray area (no pun intended), then this chapter might provide something of value that could sway you one way or the other. If – like the majority of people – you claim that in no way there can be aliens from another star system visiting us (either now or in the past), then you would be courageous if you examined your current paradigm. Consider, for a moment, that you might be a modern version of a Patagonian native and face the possibility that your "reality tunnel" indeed might be a bit narrow. Yes, be brave and read on! This takes courage and is not for weaker intellects. A paradigm shift might be uncomfortable, as they always are, but it will ultimately serve you well.

Is there such a thing as global warming? Is there such a thing as alien beings from outer space? Are these nothing more than societal (or personal) fantasies designed to serve an agenda, or do they in fact represent a serious problem? Of course, these are in no way meant to be synonymous – one could easily be true without the other, but both could pose very serious problems if we do not address them. Most of the skeptics, however, seem to have embraced the attitude of, "Don't confuse me with facts or evidence – my mind is made up."

My First UFO Experience

This material may upset you. I could not have handled these events in my twenties or thirties; but in my forties, I was ready for new experiences. I had my first experience with UFOs in Sedona, Arizona in the late 1980s. It was here that I met Virgil Postlethwaite (aka Virgil "Posti" Armstrong), who was there investigating UFOs for the CIA. Of course I did not know this when I first met him at talk he had given.

I made a comment to him after one of his lectures. Although I do not recall the context, I said:

"It is claimed in the last book of the Bible, The Book of Revelation, that all of the evil spirits will be lined up in front of the Lake of Fire to be thrown in. I think this is a test to see if we have developed enough compassion. If we allow those beings to be thrown into the Lake of Fire, we fail the test."

He was so struck by this that he responded with, "Stay in Sedona. We just might have some experiences that will change your life." He claimed that he wanted to get my take on any experiences we had.

We went to what is called the Apache Wells vortex area. There Virgil and I hiked up the steep mountainside. He, despite being twelve years older than I, was in much better shape. He claimed that three invisible ships were hovering above us. I suddenly thought I had made a mistake by coming with him. Then I began to notice strange lights appearing on the hills far below us. These lights shifted and moved from side to side, and I was immediately awestruck.

The sun's setting forced us to climb down the steep hill in near darkness. At one point I sprained my ankle pretty badly. He put his hands on my ankle and looked off in the direction of "the ships." Immediately, I felt a powerful relief from the excruciating pain and found that I could walk again. As we finally approached the car, I sensed the pain returning. Now it really hurt again.

Virgil left me in a motel room in Sedona, and I kept hearing strange noises in the room. I finally addressed the noises, saying, "Leave me alone: I can't take any more." My paradigm for new experiences was definitely on overload. I left the room to see the great Al Pacino movie, *And Justice for All*. I needed something like this to calm my nerves. I hardly slept that night.

After I got to know Virgil better, he mentioned that more than eighty government operatives were investigating UFOs at the time. He said he made about $80,000 a year, plus expenses, by investigating something the American government claims does not exist.

On my way back to my home in Los Angeles, I had a strong feeling that I should stop my car and get out. I was in the middle of nowhere in the Anza-Borrego desert. I was resistant to this because my ankle still hurt. Finally, after more prodding from this very strong feeling, I eventually stopped the car and got out. Immediately, over a hill in the distance, a UFO appeared. That lasted only for a couple of minutes and eventually the UFO went back to wherever it had come from.

Bob Lazar

Bob Lazar claims to have worked at Area 51 and has revealed a great deal of interesting information regarding work done there to back-engineer advanced alien craft. The government "damage control" units are trying to convince those who believe Lazar's testimony to see him as a big fake. My awareness of these government accusations only causes me to want to investigate him further. While there, Lazar says he experienced many amazing things.

First of all, he claims that he saw an alien there. This in itself does not prove anything. For me, however, it is more evidence toward the validity of what I have personally witnessed.

Bob also claims that he worked on a "substance" called Element 115 – something supposedly used to power these craft that modern chemistry has not yet discovered.

He also states that he walked into a large hangar and found nine different alien UFOs – all in various sizes. He called one of them "the sports model." Lazar blew the whistle in 1989, soon after he was caught bringing civilians to the outskirts of the base late at night to witness test flights. Once caught, he claims his records were erased and he basically became a "non-person," unable to prove virtually any connection to his previous job. Since then, he has been a frequent guest on the Art Bell and George Noory radio talk shows.

I heard Lazar when he appeared on these shows. He sounded legitimate to me. That, however, was not convincing enough. Conviction would come only from my own personal experiences with UFOs. I still had the nagging belief that these UFOs might actually be military; however, that opinion changed when I began interviewing people who claimed to have been abducted by aliens.

Further Proof

Some researchers claim that two to five million people in the United States have been abducted by aliens. Most retain no memory of the events, which is by design. But every one of those who remember these traumatic, life-changing events suddenly have no problem believing in alien beings.

As mentioned earlier, when I had dinner with a group of alien abductees, I was informed that I was the only one at the table who had not experienced an alien abduction. My first thought was that I was sitting with crazy people; yet all of these people seemed quite rational. My first surprise came from the consistency of the stories: they all experienced virtually the same frightening events – right down to the same details, despite the fact that they came from different areas of the country. They were gracious in sharing their experiences once I had established that I knew nothing about alien abductions and was interested in learning more. These people were not New Age "fruit cakes" who only saw love and light in all circumstances. They were *all* sharp, professional people who led responsible lives.

My Other UFO Experiences

I was fortunate enough to have witnessed a UFO landing, yet seeing it from a distance was still not convincing enough for me. To gain satisfaction, I had to hike alone through mountainous terrain to the spot where I thought it landed. This was in the Laguna Mountain area, sixty miles east of San Diego. After an exhausting and potentially fruitless search, I finally came upon three deep triangular depressions in the ground. I had found evidence that gave validity to the sighting. Although I rode out there with two women, Marti and Dolly, neither of them would hike with me. Maybe they were afraid of what they might have seen. Many people, when confronted with the chance to disrupt their current paradigm, will suddenly refuse. In the case of these two women, however, they said they had seen this before so declined.

On this night Marti, Dolly, and I had a number of UFO experiences. Marti claimed she originally contacted me because she had received my name and number through a channeling session with "the space brothers." ("Oh, sure!" I thought then.) I met the two of them for the first time when I rode in the car with them. We got to know each other as we drove the sixty miles east from San Diego. Upon arrival in the Laguna Wilderness, we saw a light in the sky a short distance from the road we were driving on.

I told them that I didn't think it was a UFO. As if on cue, the "light" started moving toward us. I was afraid that the light was going to crash because it was moving not over the trees *but actually through them.* "Sparks" were flying all over the place. I feared that I wouldn't have anything intelligent to say to "the aliens" or whoever was in the "craft" if they picked us up. However, the light kept going through the trees until it eventually disappeared over a distant mountain.

We saw many strange things in the sky that evening – one of the strangest happened about midnight. Blazing purple lights in the sky hovered above us. Then they took off at a speed that I could not even guess at. Dolly and Marti estimated they were going about 10,000 miles an hour. While I was awestruck by everything I saw, the two women took it all in stride: they had been here and seen all this before. Knowing that I was a writer and journalist, they had just wanted to have me along and get my take on the events. When it seemed a craft had landed over a nearby hill, I was off and running.

One night with one of those women, Marti, I had another strange experience involving UFOs. Marti and I had consumed between us a half-gallon of wine. I have only been "drunk" four times in my life, and most of the time I don't consume alcohol at all, so it doesn't take much of it to bring my sobriety into question. Thus, when we saw lights in the sky, we were juiced enough to be uncommonly bold and crass. The UFO appeared to be hiding behind a group of trees.

"I see you, motherfucker! Come on out and show yourself!" I screamed. This was in an area so isolated that I was sure no one else could hear us.

"Reveal yourself, you assholes!" Marti yelled.

"I'm getting impatient. Patience is not one of my virtues!" I informed this possible extraterrestrial machine.

We were so incredibly "brave" that we could barely stand up. Eventually, the light moved out from the cluster of trees. It moved slowly in our direction. When it moved within about 150 feet of us, it changed itself into a small hovering plane and began making some very strange "raspberry" noises.

"*Very funny!*" Marti yelled.

Marti and I had both experienced UFO activity, but this was the only time that a UFO revealed that it – or its probable non-human inhabitants – had a sense of humor.

On another night in another place (Arizona's Superstition Mountains), a group of good friends and I were out "UFO hunting." After a long wait, a strange light appeared in the sky.

Norma, a free spirit if I ever saw one, called out to the UFO:

"Come on, Space Brothers, come on down and make my tits bigger."

Evidently, the Space Brothers weren't into expanding bust sizes that night, so they just flew over and ignored us.

However, it was one night in the Laguna Mountains of Southern California that the alleged Space Brothers put on a "light show" for me and my close friends, Beverly and Richard Hutchinson. UFOs of varying colors nearly filled the skies. Big black UFOs went directly above us and danced in erratic patterns. There was not a time when UFOs were absent. Because we needed to get some sleep and were about a two-hour drive from my San Diego home, we had to leave the area. Some UFOs followed us as we drove from the isolated area back to the freeway toward San Diego.

The next week, Richard and Beverly brought their parents and two close friends from Anaheim to see the UFOs – but I guess they (the UFOs) were not in the mood. Nothing really happened – except for one lone light that went through a tree and sent sparks flying. No one could explain what that was. To us, the previous visitors, this wasn't much compared to last time. But it was amazing enough for the others to create the following circumstance: Richard and Beverly's close friends, Patti and Bob, never spoke to them again. Be sure that you don't mess with people's comfort zones; they may not ever forgive you.

Because of the amazing things I was experiencing, friends Don and Jane Thompson became curious and went with me to the Laguna Mountains. (Jane is the pastor's wife mentioned earlier who referred to God as "She." Don believed that he has indeed been called by God to be a minister.) All of us experienced some amazing UFOs, from giant black ones hovering above us, to multi-colored lights coming over the fields where we were standing. When a simple white light followed us back to the freeway, Don and Jane "booed" it because it was inferior to what we had seen earlier that evening.

The following week I received a post card from Don that said, "What do I do now?"

One of the things I learned is that there is a certain protocol expected when watching UFOs. For example, don't bring a camera to any potential UFO sighting. That is one way to guarantee that you will not see anything.

I took Steve and Scott, two members of the college church group I was working with, out to the Laguna Mountains. As soon as a UFO manifested, Steve produced a hidden camera. The UFO immediately disappeared, and we didn't see anything else that evening. Whether this was a cause-effect situation or not, I don't know.

I have seen many UFOs and urge readers to seek *experiences* rather than beliefs. I cover this in greater depth in *Freedom from Religion*. Because I sought experience rather than belief, I have seen more than my share of UFOs. Thus, I no longer need to be convinced. I leave that for the belief junkies and the religious "true believers."

However, some people will never be convinced no matter how much evidence you give them – including direct experiences with UFOs. In a discussion with Valerie and Chris, two women from my college-age youth group, I sensed a real resistance from Valerie. She said, "Jack, you don't understand. I don't need any proof. I know that everything is perfect and that we don't need to do anything. I don't need to see your UFOs."

A Different Kind of Dinner

On a Monday Night in Walnut Creek, California, a group of six people gathered at a Marie Callenders restaurant. Unlike my previous session where everyone at the table was an alien abductee, what this group had in common was that everyone at the table believed that there were indeed aliens on planet Earth and that they might pose a threat to society.

The conversation was refreshing. No judgment toward others, just open minds that listened. No need to think about what one should say or how to say it.

One of the members of this group had a difficult time dealing with the fact that whoever was doing the cattle mutilations was also doing the same things to people's pets. She was a passionate animal lover, and this reality seemed to upset her.

I had brought a book I had promised for one of the group to read: Ingo Swann's *Penetration*. This dealt with not only what Swann experienced while remote viewing the back side of the moon, but also the fact that most remote viewers have experienced aliens in their "journeys."

That evening, none of us needed any proof. In fact, I felt I could relate the stories about my UFO experiences safely, without being considered strange or even crazy.

Each of us expressed frustration in dealing with our friends: we simply could not talk about the aliens as freely as we wished. If we tried, we were considered "whacked out" or (even worse) irrelevant. If indeed there are aliens here in Earth's airspace, the bulk of humanity is aiding them by their ignorance, allowing the aliens to operate in relative safety. Thus, the dozens of UFOs witnessed in my life are considered, by the general masses, to be basically irrelevant. With the current mindset of the masses, whatever plans the aliens have in mind for us might be brought to fruition with little or no resistance. Should they decide (as in the past) that they want to be worshiped again, or to control us again, they will most likely be successful.

When they land, we will all finally see the aliens and the small craft that they use to go short distances. Yet most of us might experience the same circumstance Magellan encountered with the native Patagonians: we may not see or understand the big ship.

Subscribe to FATE Magazine Today!

- Ancient Mysteries
- Alien Abductions
- UFOs
- Atlantis
- Alternative Archaeology
- Lost Civilizations
- And more ...

FATE covers it all like no else. Published since 1948, FATE is the longest-running publication of its kind in the world, supplying its loyal readers with a broad array of true accounts of the strange and unknown for more than 63 years. FATE is a full-color, 120-page, bimonthly magazine that brings you exciting, in-depth coverage of the world's mysterious and unexplained phenomena.

1-year subscription only $27.95
Call 1-800-728-2730 or visit *www.fatemag.com*

Green Subscriptions. E-issues.
Only $39.95 for the entire year!
Go green. Save a tree, and save money.

12 issues of FATE delivered electronically to your computer for less than $3.95 an issue. • Receive twice as many issues as a print subscription. Includes six regular issues plus six theme issues (UFOs; Ghosts; Cryptozoology & Monsters; Nature Spirits & Spirituality; Strange Places & Sacred Sites; and Life After Death). • Free membership in FATE E-club (save $10). • Free all-access to Hilly Rose shows (save $12.95). • Members-only video interviews. • Discounts on all FATE merchandise. • Monthly Special Offers.

Made in the USA
Middletown, DE
30 March 2023